# PREFACE

## 1. Scope

This publication provides doctrine for planning, coordinating, and conducting joint shipboard helicopter and tiltrotor aircraft operations from United States air-capable ships.

## 2. Purpose

This publication has been prepared under the direction of the Chairman of the Joint Chiefs of Staff. It sets forth joint doctrine to govern the activities and performance of the Armed Forces of the United States in joint operations and provides the doctrinal basis for US military coordination with other US Government departments and agencies during operations and for US military involvement in multinational operations. It provides military guidance for use by the Armed Forces in preparing their appropriate plans. It is not the intent of this publication to restrict the authority of the joint force commander (JFC) from organizing the force and executing the mission in a manner the JFC deems most appropriate to ensure unity of effort in the accomplishment of the overall objective.

## 3. Application

a. Joint doctrine established in this publication applies to the Joint Staff, commanders of combatant commands, subordinate unified commands, joint task forces, subordinate components of these commands, and the Services.

b. The guidance in this publication is authoritative; as such, this doctrine will be followed except when, in the judgment of the commander, exceptional circumstances dictate otherwise. If conflicts arise between the contents of this publication and the contents of Service publications, this publication will take precedence unless the Chairman of the Joint Chiefs of Staff, normally in coordination with the other members of the Joint Chiefs of Staff, has provided more current and specific guidance. Commanders of forces operating as part of a multinational (alliance or coalition) military command should follow multinational doctrine and procedures ratified by the United States. For doctrine and procedures not ratified by the United States, commanders should evaluate and follow the multinational command's doctrine and procedures, where applicable and consistent with US law, regulations, and doctrine.

For the Chairman of the Joint Chiefs of Staff:

CURTIS M. SCAPARROTTI
Lieutenant General, U.S. Army
Director, Joint Staff

Intentionally Blank

## SUMMARY OF CHANGES
### JOINT PUBLICATION 3-04
### DATED 30 SEPTEMBER 2008

- Adds information to rotor weight classifications.

- Adds the term "tiltrotor aircraft" with "helicopter" throughout the publication.

- Updates and harmonizes discussion of safety concerns for aircraft passengers and troop movement.

- Updates discussion for flight and hangar deck operations.

- Updates "Shipboard Helicopter/Tiltrotor Aircraft Deck Handling/Movement" section to accurately reflect extant capabilities, procedures, and processes.

- Updates the current references.

- Glossary has been significantly revised by deleting outdated terms, modifying and adding a number of definitions, and properly sourcing all terms.

Intentionally Blank

# TABLE OF CONTENTS

GLOSSARY

FIGURE

- **Describes the Unique Aspects of Joint Shipboard Helicopter and Tiltrotor Aircraft Operations**

- **Describes Pre-Deployment, Embarkation, and Debarkation Planning for Joint Shipboard Helicopter and Tiltrotor Aircraft Operations**

- **Addresses Operations, Shipboard Command Authorities, and Flight and Hangar Deck Operations**

- **Covers Sustainment Responsibilities**

---

### Introduction to Joint Shipboard Helicopter and Tiltrotor Aircraft Operations

*This publication provides general guidance for integrating any Service helicopter or tiltrotor aircraft onboard air-capable ships, amphibious assault ships, and aircraft carriers for operations from the sea.*

Unlike some joint operations where the Services are assigned operational areas and interact with each other on the margins (via communications channels or across boundary lines), joint shipboard helicopter and tiltrotor operations require continuous interaction, coordination, and teamwork to accomplish the simplest of tasks. Poor interaction and coordination can result in personnel injury and equipment damage. If not quickly identified and mitigated, Service differences in terminology, training, equipment, and standing operating procedures will be magnified and may develop into significant challenges.

### Planning

*Joint Force Commander Considerations*

When embarking other Service helicopters/tiltrotor aircraft on Navy ships, there are three major ship mission trade-offs to consider: displacement of naval aircraft; removal of the ship from its place in the amphibious ready group or carrier strike group; and degradation of ship and/or embarked unit mission capabilities resulting from emission control (EMCON)/hazards of electromagnetic radiation to ordnance (HERO) requirements, wind limitations, and/or geographic location requirements. Joint force commander (JFC) considerations also include the impact of embarking other Service helicopters or tiltrotor aircraft on a small air-capable ship (ACS) (such as a cruiser or destroyer) or on an aircraft carrier or amphibious assault ship.

**Compatibility Analysis**

*When helicopters/tiltrotor aircraft are embarked aboard ships with flight decks, physical incompatibilities can have a negative impact on the operational capabilities of both the ship and the embarking unit.*

After determining the desired mission capabilities, it is necessary to determine whether the desired mix of ships, helicopters, and tiltrotor aircraft to achieve that mission are compatible. It is incumbent upon the personnel of the embarking unit and the ship to analyze potential incompatibilities and take actions to minimize them in advance of operations. Factors to consider include:

- Geometric fit/deck load limits
- Rotorcraft weight classifications
- Helicopter/tiltrotor aircraft characteristics/limitations
- Electromagnetic environmental effects
- Ordnance
- Ship and helicopter/tiltrotor aircraft major equipment/servicing interoperability
- Shipboard refueling

**General Planning Considerations**

*General planning considerations include mission integration, ordnance planning, command and control planning, operations, logistics and supply, vertical takeoff and landing unmanned aircraft system.*

Regardless of the time available for planning, the following areas must be considered: administration, required training and certification, embarkation, communications system support, intelligence operations, health services, ordnance, helicopter maintenance, and logistics/supply. Typically, when United States Army or United States Air Force units embark aboard ship the personnel of both the embarking unit and the ship have limited knowledge of each other's capabilities and operational concepts.

**Pre-Deployment Training and Certification**

Pilots obtain initial, recurrent, and requalification training for type aircraft in accordance with parent Service directives as appropriate. Before embarkation, helicopter/tiltrotor aircraft detachments will be certified for shipboard operations by their unit commander or other authority.

**Embarkation Planning**

*Embarkation planning involves reverse planning from the objective, to the landing zone, to the ship, and to the port of embarkation such that the equipment that will be needed first is the last*

There are several avenues for onload of personnel and equipment. For small units, embarking for short duration, flying everything aboard may be the preferred method. For larger units or for longer durations, a combination of pierside loading and fly-on may be the optimal method. Ordnance can be loaded pierside or flown aboard the ship while underway as cargo. Coordination of fly-on from a shore site to a ship at sea will depend on distance between the ship and shore, available navigation aids, and communications between shore air traffic control (ATC)

*equipment loaded onboard ship.*

and the ship's controllers. Several items should be coordinated and agreed upon before flying out to the ship (e.g., arrival sequence, ship's position, navigational aids [NAVAIDS]).

*Debarkation Planning*

There are two debarkation processes to discuss. **Mission debarkation** is leaving the ship to conduct the mission (return to the ship is anticipated and expected) and is focused on operational concerns and support requirements. **Post-mission debarkation** is leaving the ship (return not anticipated). Embarked helicopter/tiltrotor aircraft may fly off the ship as it approaches port or in some cases may fly off the ship once it is pierside. When arranging to fly off, helicopter/tiltrotor aircraft units should ensure coordination among ATC (both ship and shore), the ship's operations and air departments, and unit shore personnel. Issues to consider prior to fly-off include departure sequence, ship's position, NAVAIDS, etc.

*Safety*

*The squadron commanding officer or detachment officer in charge and ship personnel will evaluate the hazards involved in all phases of shipboard helicopter/ tiltrotor aircraft operations and develop appropriate safety measures.*

The commanding officer (CO) of the ship has supervisory responsibility for the safety of embarked helicopters/tiltrotor aircraft at all times. The helicopter/tiltrotor aircraft unit CO or detachment officer in charge (OIC) and the individual aircraft pilots are directly responsible for the safety of assigned aircraft and personnel. In questionable circumstances, the embarked unit CO or detachment OIC will make the final determination concerning flight safety of aircraft, crew, and passengers.

*Ordnance*

The movement, handling, and stowage of explosive ordnance carried aboard ships and aircraft is inherently dangerous. Shipboard handling/stowage of ammunition/explosives is therefore governed by the most definitive and restrictive Department of Defense regulations and precautions. Safety must not be jeopardized by either the introduction of weapons not approved for shipboard employment by Weapon System Explosive Safety Review Board/Chief of Naval Operations or use of inadequately trained personnel to accomplish explosive tasks.

*Electromagnetic Environmental Effects*

Operations in and around ships subject both the helicopter/tiltrotor aircraft and the ship to electromagnetic environmental effects emissions neither may have been designed to encounter. When planning shipboard helicopter/tiltrotor operations, potential radiation hazards, electromagnetic interference, and electronic vulnerability effects must be considered so that applicable transmitter conditions can be set prior to arrival of helicopters/tiltrotor aircraft aboard the ship. Planners should contact the Joint Spectrum Center to receive proper HERO and electromagnetic vulnerability guidance prior to issuing authorization to conduct helicopter/tiltrotor aircraft operations.

## Operations

*Pre-Operations*

Operational effectiveness and flight safety require extensive training in the areas of command and control, aircraft coordination, and flight deck procedures. Units such as special operations forces that desire a special compartment information facility for planning should make this requirement known early in the pre-deployment planning process as these facilities are limited in number and size, particularly on ACS. Some embarked units will bring their own portable communications equipment. Possible interference with shipboard electronics and EMCON policies must be considered and carefully coordinated.

*Shipboard Command Authorities*

United States Navy and United States Coast Guard regulations set forth the authority of the ship's CO with respect to aircraft embarked in or operating from the ship. An embarked unit commander/detachment OIC shall be designated by the JFC or the parent unit's CO. The designated commander/OIC reports directly to the ship's CO, air wing commander, or authority specified by the JFC for the mission assigned. Administratively, the commander/OIC normally reports to the ship's executive officer for matters of day-to-day routine with respect to the embarked unit while embarked on the ship.

*Flight and Hangar Deck Operations*

*Limited space and the potential for conducting numerous varied and hazardous tasks simultaneously require close control and coordination to*

All post-landing events will be controlled by/coordinated with appropriate ship's personnel. After coordination has been accomplished, the ship will provide a qualified move director and move crew. The helicopter/tiltrotor aircraft unit will provide a plane captain or crew chief to act as a brake rider and/or unit safety observer. Based upon the air plan and flight schedule, the ship will man its flight quarters stations in time to meet the first scheduled launch. Each ship and embarked unit should establish the

*ensure that operations are conducted safely.*

pre-takeoff sequence that best supports their operations and the assigned mission. Helicopter/tiltrotor aircraft engines/auxiliary power units shall not be started without the ship's permission. During initial engine start and rotor engagement, the low inertia/speed of the main helicopter rotor blades will permit rotor blades to flex and flap as they rotate. Caution should be observed during this stage of rotor engagement to keep personnel outside and well clear of the rotor arc.

## Sustainment

*Deck Handling/ Maneuvering/Spotting*

Space is very limited aboard ship, with aircraft required to share takeoff, landing, and maintenance spots. Helicopters designed for land operations typically require more space than helicopters designed for maritime operations. Personnel are trained to maneuver embarked maritime helicopters/tiltrotor aircraft using the support equipment embarked. It may be necessary to alter established practices when using shipboard support equipment with helicopter/tiltrotor aircraft designed for land operations because of their limitations and compatibility with shipboard configurations.

*Maintenance Considerations*

Most shipboard helicopter/tiltrotor aircraft maintenance must be conducted on the flight deck of the ship. Flight decks are exposed to the elements and are in constant motion due to changing sea states. As a result, helicopter/tiltrotor aircraft maintenance can be extremely hazardous at all times, but especially at night, in inclement weather, or when flight operations are in progress. Each class/type ship has different helicopter/tiltrotor aircraft maintenance support capabilities and procedures.

*Other Logistics and Personnel Service Considerations*

A short-duration detachment will usually draw the bulk of its supply material from a packup kit provided by the parent Service. Resupply of drawn material will occur as needed. Material support for detachments of longer duration will be better served by establishing an independent unit identity, especially when shipboard operations will be conducted outside the umbrella of the parent Service support infrastructure. Establishment of independent unit identity will provide the most flexible support if a helicopter/tiltrotor aircraft unit is to relocate from ship-to-ship or ship-to-shore.

## CONCLUSION

This publication provides doctrine for planning, coordinating, and conducting joint shipboard helicopter and tiltrotor aircraft operations from United States ACSs.

# CHAPTER I
## INTRODUCTION TO JOINT SHIPBOARD HELICOPTER AND TILTROTOR AIRCRAFT OPERATIONS

*"The helicopter is probably the most versatile instrument ever invented by man. It approaches closer than any other to fulfillment of mankind's ancient dreams of the flying horse and the magic carpet."*

**Igor Sikorsky, 13 September 1959**

## 1. Purpose

a. This publication provides general guidance for integrating any Service helicopter or tiltrotor aircraft onboard air-capable ships (ACSs), amphibious assault ships (AASs), and aircraft carriers for operations from the sea.

b. Authoritative multi-Service and Service publications containing technical data, safety of flight information, and other guidance subject to periodic reviews are appropriately referenced throughout this publication. A comprehensive listing of relevant references is provided in Appendix A, "Shipboard Helicopter and Tiltrotor Operations Publications."

## 2. General

a. Each ship class is different in this regard; however, all aspects of the ship must be shared such as command and control (C2) facilities, office spaces, maintenance spaces, flight deck, hangar deck, medical and dental facilities, storage areas, logistics, messing, and berthing. Unlike some joint operations where the Services are assigned operational areas and interact with each other on the margins (via communications channels or across boundary lines), joint shipboard helicopter and tiltrotor operations require continuous interaction, coordination, and teamwork to accomplish the simplest of tasks. Poor interaction and coordination can result in personnel injury and equipment damage. If not quickly identified and mitigated, Service differences in terminology, training, equipment, and standing operating procedures will be magnified and may develop into significant challenges.

b. A ship provides the combined benefits of a landing zone, maintenance and work areas, refueling platform, air operations planning facilities, and C2. The ship also provides for sustainment, living, dining, and recreation provisions, as well as other daily necessities such as the ship's laundry, store, and barber shop.

c. Above all else, the shipboard environment demands the ultimate in teamwork. At any time there can be an event, combat-related or otherwise (e.g., heavy weather), that may affect all personnel aboard the ship. Even during peacetime, the ever-present dangers of flooding or fire can require sounding "general quarters (GQ)" which stations the crew (including helicopter/tiltrotor aircraft detachments) to an assigned battle station. It is important to understand the potential lethality of the flight deck environment during flight operations. If an aircraft mishap occurs, there is the real possibility of a major conflagration because of the explosive characteristics of fuel and ordnance that, if not properly responded to, may cause the loss of ship and lives. It is incumbent on everyone embarked on a ship to know their responsibilities during the many evolutions that transpire during normal ship's routine. The ship's company (crew) has the responsibility to impart that knowledge to personnel not familiar with ship surroundings.

d. Daily shipboard routine is promulgated in the ship's plan of the day (POD). The POD is the primary means of announcing each day's schedule of important events and will normally include the daily flight schedule on non-ACSs, whereas on ACSs, it will be promulgated as a daily air plan. The ship's executive officer (XO) is responsible for the POD. Commanders and officers in charge (OICs) of embarked units should be included in POD development to better coordinate the use of common spaces, accommodate training activities, synchronize operations, and ensure that their unit's personnel fully understand shipboard responsibilities. For information that needs to be passed to the crew in a timely fashion, there is a general announcing system (1MC).

e. General shipboard helicopter/tiltrotor aircraft operations and procedures as well as specific mission tactics are not covered in this publication. Consult the source documents listed in Appendix A, "Shipboard Helicopter and Tiltrotor Operations Publications" for specific procedures. Wind envelopes (the wind limits for individual helicopter/tiltrotor aircraft and ship combinations) are contained in the following Naval Air Training and Operating Procedures Standardization (NATOPS) program publications and Commandant, United States Coast Guard (USCG), instruction (COMDTINST):

(1) Naval Air Systems Command (NAVAIR) 00-80T-105, *CV NATOPS Manual.*

(2) NAVAIR 00-80T-106, *LHA/LHD NATOPS Manual.*

(3) NAVAIR 00-80T-122, *Helicopter Operating Procedures for Air-Capable Ships NATOPS Manual.*

(4) NAVAIR A1-V22AB-NFM-000, *NATOPS Flight Manual Navy Model MV-22B Tiltrotor.*

(5) NAVAIR A1-V22AC-AFM-000, *NATOPS Flight Manual USAF Series CV-22 Tiltrotor.*

(6) COMDTINST M3710.2, *Shipboard-Helicopter Operational Procedures Manual.*

f. If there is a conflict between authoritative technical manuals and the information in this publication, the technical manual will take precedence.

# CHAPTER II
# PLANNING

## 1. Joint Force Commander Considerations

a. **Mission Trade-offs.** When embarking other Service helicopters/tiltrotor aircraft on Navy ships, there are three major ship mission trade-offs to consider:

(1) Displacement of naval aircraft.

(2) Removal of the ship from its place in the amphibious ready group (ARG) or carrier strike group in order to support the embarked unit.

(3) Degradation of ship and/or embarked unit mission capabilities resulting from emission control (EMCON)/hazards of electromagnetic radiation to ordnance (HERO) requirements, wind limitations, and/or geographic location requirements.

b. The impact of embarking other Service helicopters or tiltrotor aircraft on a small ACS (such as a cruiser or destroyer) is relatively easy to assess because their traditional missions such as antisubmarine warfare or ballistic missile defense are rather straightforward.

c. The impact of embarking other Service helicopters/tiltrotor aircraft on an aircraft carrier (CV) or AAS is usually more difficult to assess because the ships are complex, multi-mission platforms.

(1) If the footprint of embarking unit's helicopters/tiltrotor aircraft, when added to the carrier air wing (CVW)/aviation combat element (ACE) footprint, is larger than the maximum allowable ship deck density, some CVW or ACE aircraft will have to be debarked.

(2) The number of other Service helicopters/tiltrotor aircraft embarked, including associated equipment and personnel and the anticipated duration of the embarkation, drive mission area trade-offs.

(a) The number and type of helicopters/tiltrotor aircraft and numbers and ranks/rates of personnel will determine the number of naval aircraft and personnel that must be debarked to make room for the embarking units.

(b) Lost maritime mission capabilities may result from disruptions in normal flight operations and maintenance or having to debark a significant number of ship aircraft and personnel.

d. **Large Scale Helicopter/Tiltrotor Aircraft Operations.** For large-scale operations involving battalion or brigade size aviation units, aircraft carriers, AASs and/or multispot ships are required. Flight decks can only accommodate a limited number of helicopters/tiltrotor aircraft. Folding rotor blades will increase the number of helicopters/tiltrotor aircraft that may be embarked on a particular ship. However, manually folded rotor blades require more time to spread in order to launch the helicopter/tiltrotor aircraft and may make mission accomplishment more difficult. On large deck ships it is possible to develop alternate spotting schemes that will accommodate large numbers of helicopters/tiltrotor aircraft and that do not require blades to be folded. Contact Naval Air Warfare Center, Aircraft Division (NAWCAD) Lakehurst, New Jersey, for assistance and approval of nonstandard spotting plans. The choreography required for high deck density operations necessitates meticulous planning. Cyclic flight operations can be planned and coordinated for operations from several ships simultaneously. Among the issues to consider are:

(1) Wave/serial composition.

(2) Distance to the landing zone/target area.

(3) Time required to respot the deck for the next wave/serial.

(4) Arrangements for a helicopter/tiltrotor aircraft requiring an emergency landing.

e. **Ship/Unit Capabilities and Limitations.** To effectively plan helicopter or tiltrotor operations, the embarking unit's planner should be familiar with the various classifications of ship aviation capabilities.

(1) **Air-Capable Flight Deck Information.** US air-capable flight deck information is contained in the annually updated Naval Air Engineering Center–Engineering (NAEC-ENG)-7576, *Shipboard Aviation Facilities Resume,* produced by NAWCAD, Lakehurst. This document describes and depicts aircraft landing, vertical replenishment (VERTREP)/hover, and helicopter in-flight refueling (HIFR) facilities aboard ACSs. HIFR, not to be confused with helicopter aerial refueling, is the practice of refueling a hovering helicopter from a fuel hose attached to the flight deck. The data is compiled from aviation facility certification inspection team reports.

(2) **Air-Capable Ships.** Most ships are classified as ACSs, which are characterized by small flight decks on the stern, bow, or both. Due to the size of some smaller flight decks, certain helicopters/tiltrotor aircraft are limited to hover operations only. The number of helicopter/tiltrotor aircraft landing spots available to support operations should be verified prior to embarkation. ACSs are divided into three levels which describe the environmental conditions in which each ship is capable of operating.

(a) Level I ships are capable of operations day or night, in visual meteorological conditions (VMC) or instrument meteorological conditions (IMC), and are equipped with tactical air navigation (TACAN) and ultrahigh frequency (UHF) homing.

(b) Level II ships are capable of day or night, VMC operations only.

(c) Level III ships are capable of day, VMC operations only.

(d) Each level is further divided into seven classes which describes the specific type helicopter/tiltrotor aircraft support capability of each ship:

1. Class 1 ships provide landing clearance, a hangar, fuel and electrical service, and full maintenance facilities.

2. Class 2 ships provide landing clearance plus fuel and electrical service.

3. Class 2A ships provide landing clearance plus fuel and direct current electrical service.

4. Class 3 ships provide landing clearance.

5. Class 4 ships provide hover clearance down to 5 feet.

6. Class 5 ships provide hover clearance above 15 feet.

7. Class 6 ships provide HIFR.

*Refer to NAVAIR 00-80T-122,* Helicopter Operating Procedures for Air-Capable Ships NATOPS Manual, *for detailed procedures when operating with Navy ACS or to COMDTINST M3710.2,* Shipboard-Helicopter Operational Procedures Manual.

(3) **Amphibious Assault Ships.** The Navy has two ship classes which fall into this category: amphibious assault ship (general purpose) (LHA), and amphibious assault ship (multipurpose) (LHD). These ships are characterized by large flight decks with multiple landing spots, a large hangar below the flight deck, and full maintenance and service capabilities. These ships are day and night all-helicopter, tiltrotor aircraft (short takeoff and vertical landing aircraft), and vertical/short takeoff and landing operations capable, aided by TACAN and full radar services from the helicopter direction center (HDC)/amphibious air traffic control center (AATCC). Refer to NAVAIR 00-80T-106, *LHA/LHD NATOPS Manual,* for detailed procedures when operating with AASs.

(4) **Aircraft Carriers.** Aircraft carriers, nuclear (CVNs), are the only ships in this category. Helicopters/tiltrotor aircraft can expect full services and maintenance support when operating from aircraft carriers. The carrier air traffic control (ATC) center provides complete radar service in all weather, day and night. Refer to NAVAIR 00-80T-105, *CV*

*NATOPS Manual,* and NAVAIR 00-80T-120, *CV NATOPS for Flight Deck and Hangar Deck,* for detailed procedures when operating with aircraft carriers.

## 2. Compatibility Analysis

After determining the desired mission capabilities, it is necessary to determine whether the desired mix of ships, helicopters, and tiltrotor aircraft to achieve that mission are compatible. If there are incompatibilities, then planning their integration must include mitigation efforts.

a. **General.** When helicopters/tiltrotor aircraft are embarked aboard ships with flight decks, physical incompatibilities can have a negative impact on the operational capabilities of both the ship and the embarking unit. It is incumbent upon the personnel of the embarking unit and the ship to analyze potential incompatibilities and take actions to minimize them in advance of operations. Failure to do so can lead to significant operational problems, damage to equipment, and/or injury to personnel. Factors to consider include:

(1) Severely limited space for flight operations, maintenance, and storage.

(2) High power electromagnetic (EM) emitters operating in close proximity to aircraft and personnel and HERO.

(3) Limited options for alternate landing sites.

(4) Heightened fire risks due to crowded conditions and proximity of ordnance.

(5) Varying and sometimes severe ship motion.

(6) Frequent high, turbulent winds.

(7) Frequently obscured or indistinct horizon IMC.

(8) Exposure of equipment to the corrosive effects of salt spray.

(9) Sudden loss of ground effect.

(10) Helicopter/tiltrotor aircraft limits (rotor engage/disengage, launch/recovery/pitch/roll).

(11) Lack of overwater navigation aids (automatic direction finder, nondirectional beacon, high frequency homing, etc.).

(12) Tiltrotor high exhaust temperatures can cause long-term fatigue damage to flight decks without proper mitigation.

(13) Electromagnetic interference (EMI) from SPS-40 and SPS-49 radars during tiltrotor blade fold wing stow.

b. Once the personnel of the embarking unit and the ship have researched potential incompatibilities, a formal visit to the ship by the embarking unit's maintenance, logistics, and operations personnel should be scheduled.

(1) It is imperative that the personnel of the embarking unit inspect the operating, maintenance, storage areas and supporting equipment they will use aboard ship. Quite often, additional compatibility issues will arise after the embarking unit has examined available/assigned ship facilities.

(2) The sources listed in Appendix A, "Shipboard Helicopter and Tiltrotor Operations Publications," may be useful for identifying known compatibility issues.

c. **Geometric Fit/Deck Load Limits.** Both ship and unit personnel should consider geometric fit issues during the planning process. Among the issues to consider are:

(1) Deck and elevator load limits.

(2) Flight deck, elevator, hangar deck fit (blades spread, folded, and/or removed).

(3) Takeoff and landing spots.

(4) Maintenance areas.

d. **Rotorcraft Weight Classifications.** Long range rotorcraft are designated to have a combat radius of 210 to 500 nautical miles. Note: V-22 downwash is similar to a heavy rotorcraft. V-22 will be considered a heavy rotorcraft during planning of shipboard/tiltrotor operations. The following rotorcraft classifications are based on maximum gross weight (MGW):

(1) Ultra rotorcraft: MGW > 100,000 pounds (lbs).

(2) Heavy rotorcraft: MGW > 70,000 lbs to 100,000 lbs.

(3) Medium rotorcraft: MGW 24,000 lbs to 70,000 lbs.

(4) Light rotorcraft: MGW < 24,000 lbs.

e. A detailed safety analysis involving aircraft fit and deck and elevator strength must be completed before embarking any helicopter/tiltrotor aircraft aboard a ship. The results of these analyses are used to determine ship certification levels and associated restrictions, which are published in the NAEC-ENG-7576, *Shipboard Aviation Facilities Resume*. Requests to deviate from the certification and restrictions published in the *Shipboard Aviation Facilities Resume* must be addressed to fleet commanders in the form of a waiver request. Waiver requests for the Navy should go to Commander, Naval Surface Force Pacific (Code N431D), information Commander, United States Pacific Fleet (COMUSPACFLT), for West Coast ships or to Commander, Naval Surface Force Atlantic (Code N42), and information Commander, United States Fleet Forces Command (COMUSFLTFORCOM), for East Coast ships. Waivers, if approved, will be granted by COMUSPACFLT or COMUSFLTFORCOM.

f. Contingency and crisis response operations may generate questions regarding nonstandard aircraft spotting to achieve a greater deck density or more rapid launch sequence than would otherwise be permitted. Should this situation arise, ships should contact the NAWCAD, Lakehurst, New Jersey, for assistance in analyzing nonstandard spotting. NAWCAD may have knowledge of previous operations with the proposed helicopter/tiltrotor aircraft and ship combination. NAWCAD engineers can help in resolving fit issues and determining best spotting arrangements for the proposed aircraft mix and operating concept.

g. **Helicopter/Tiltrotor Aircraft Characteristics/Limitations.** All helicopters have design limitations that affect the way they are moved and operated. The shipboard environment may require modifications to unit standard operating procedures (SOPs). The following helicopter/tiltrotor aircraft capabilities and limitations should be addressed and considered prior to conducting shipboard operations. *(Note: Most of the following can be obtained from the aircraft operator's manual or unit SOP. Some limitations may not be established. In those cases, units should refer to the manufacturer or to units with prior experience operating the same or similar helicopter aboard ship. Wind envelopes for tiltrotor aircraft are contained in V-22 NATOPS publications, as LHA/LHD class ships general and NAVAIR 00-08T122, Helicopter Operating Procedures for Air-Capable Ships NATOPS Manual; general envelopes do not apply to tiltrotor aircraft.)*

    (1) Heavy weather capability (tie down [TD] points, blade harness/TD, etc.).

    (2) Danger areas.

    (3) Blade arcs (vertical and horizontal clearances).

    (4) Engine/auxiliary power unit exhaust (velocity and temperature profile).

    (5) Rotor downwash (velocity and pattern).

    (6) Overwater safety provisions (egress system design/survival equipment).

    (7) Water landing capabilities (expected float time).

    (8) Door/window jettison.

    (9) Rafts/flotation devices.

(10) Signal devices (day, night, visual, aural).

(11) Beacon.

(12) Rescue harness.

(13) Self-contained search and rescue (SAR) capabilities (winch, spotlight).

(14) Loiter capability.

(15) Range capability.

(16) Overwater navigation capability.

(17) Wind limits (azimuth and velocity).

(18) Startup/shutdown (transient revolutions per minute [RPM]).

(19) Launch/recovery wind envelopes.

(20) Blades static (tied down and not tied down).

(21) Folding operations/blades folded.

(22) Pitch/roll limits.

(23) Rotor coast down (rotor brake equipped versus non-rotor brake equipped).

(24) Pilot and crew field of view/blind spots.

(25) Landing signalman enlisted (LSE) placement.

(26) Lighting (night vision device [NVD]).

(27) External lights (masthead, rotor tip, tail, navigation).

(28) Sling load/capability operations.

(29) Communications capability/radio configuration.

h. **Electromagnetic Environmental Effects (E3).** E3 is the impact of the electromagnetic environment (EME) upon the operational capability of military forces, equipment, systems, and platforms. It encompasses all EM disciplines, including EM compatibility and EMI; electromagnetic vulnerability (EMV); EM pulse; electronic protection, hazards of electromagnetic radiation to personnel (HERP), HERO, and hazards of electromagnetic radiation to fuels (HERF); and natural phenomena effects of lightning and precipitation static.

*For specific guidance on E3 planning, refer to paragraph 9, "Electromagnetic Environmental Effects."*

i. Planners should thoroughly research E3 emitter profiles and individual system susceptibilities for both helicopter/tiltrotor aircraft and ship and develop mitigation strategies to accommodate integration. Information on ships' emitter profiles may be obtained from the electronic warfare officer (EWO) aboard each ship. Information on helicopter/tiltrotor aircraft emitters may be found in the applicable helicopter/tiltrotor aircraft operating manual, or by contacting the embarking unit directly. Individual system susceptibilities may be available from classified sources. Using EMCON procedures and implementing HERO (ship's HERO EMCON bill) procedures when ships and helicopter/tiltrotor aircraft operate together can mitigate these issues.

j. **Ordnance.** Embarking units are required to inform the ship's ordnance handlers and weapons officers of specific ordnance they plan to embark. Navy ammunition logistics code (NALC) or Department of Defense identification code (DODIC) and the national stock number (NSN) should be used to identify ordnance. Shipboard magazines are certified to store many types of ordnance; however, some ordnance may not be compatible with a specific magazine. Ordnance compatibility issues include:

(1) Weapon System Explosive Safety Review Board (WSESRB) approval of the ordnance and containers for shipboard employment.

(2) WSESRB approval of the type, model, and/or series (T/M/S) aircraft and installed weapons systems.

(3) Magazine storage space to include ordnance storage compatibility.

(4) Loading equipment.

(5) HERO test data on ordnance designed with electrically initiated devices (EIDs) to determine safe shipboard radio frequency (RF) environments and/or required EMCON.

k. Although the ship's magazines may be certified to hold specific ordnance in the joint inventory, ordnance for the ship's weapons systems may not be compatible with embarked unit ordnance. Ship's ordnance handlers may need to reconfigure their magazine loads to accommodate other Service ordnance. Compatibility information for particular ordnance may be found in Naval Sea Systems Command (NAVSEA) Ordnance Publication (OP) 4, *Ammunition and Explosives Safety Afloat.*

*For more details concerning ordnance planning, refer to paragraph 8, "Ordnance."*

l. **Ship and Helicopter/Tiltrotor Aircraft Major Equipment/Servicing Interoperability.** Operations and maintenance planners should determine ship's service compatibility with the embarking helicopter's/tiltrotor aircraft's fuel, defuel, electrical, hydraulic, and pneumatic systems as well as any special ground support equipment (GSE) requirements. Information on the helicopter/tiltrotor aircraft systems requirements, such as electrical power voltage, phase, and amperage, or pneumatic pressures, servicing limits, and pressure fueling/defueling systems, is available in the service's aircraft operating manual. Ship's service information can be located in the NAEC-ENG-7576, *Shipboard Aviation Facilities Resume*.

m. **Shipboard Refueling.** Closed circuit refueling (CCR) nozzles, such as the Wiggins and North Atlantic Treaty Organization (NATO) high capacity nozzles, cannot be used to refuel closed circuit United States Army (USA) helicopters. The 45 pounds per square inch (psi) output of these nozzles could damage the aircraft's fuel systems, rupture tanks, and cause a fuel spill or fire. If shipboard CCR operations of USA aircraft are anticipated, the aircrew must provide refuel personnel with a USA fuel nozzle unless already included as part of the deployment pack-up equipment.

## 3. General Planning Considerations

The quality of pre-deployment planning relates directly to the success of the overall helicopter and tiltrotor operations. Historically, planning time has been limited by the emergent nature of contingency operations. Unit and staff personnel can enhance mission success by considering the issues discussed in the following paragraphs.

a. **General**

(1) **Considerations for Planning.** Regardless of the time available for planning, the following areas must be considered: administration, required training and certification, embarkation, communications system support, intelligence operations, health services, ordnance, helicopter maintenance, and logistics/supply.

(2) **Liaison Officers.** Liaison officers should be exchanged between the embarking unit's commander and ship's commanding officer (CO) as early as possible. Liaison officers should be prepared to discuss helicopter footprint, embarkation, C2, maintenance requirements, logistics, ordnance, communications system support, personnel, and habitability issues.

(3) **Pre-Deployment Planning.** Detailed pre-deployment planning is one of the most important factors for the successful and safe conduct of helicopter and tiltrotor operations and includes items that should be addressed prior to embarking. The timelines and checklists provided in this and other publications are recommendations that may be adjusted depending on the situation. Though it may be impossible to complete all the items listed in the various checklists prior to embarkation, the checklists should be used as a starting point for planning. Those items that cannot be completed prior will be accomplished shortly after embarking.

(a) The following essential elements of pre-deployment planning are addressed in this chapter and throughout this publication: presail conference, embarking unit pre-deployment checklist, embarkation conference(s), pre-embarkation ship visit(s), and training and qualification requirements (safety, fire fighting, ordnance handling, ship indoctrination, maintenance, aircrew, and deck landing qualification [DLQ]).

(b) Personnel from the units involved should meet with/talk to their counterparts as early as possible and continue a dialogue until the at-sea period is completed. It is essential to discuss integration issues prior to helicopter and tiltrotor operations.

b. **Presail Conference.** The naval surface community schedules a presail conference during the early stages of deployment planning involving an embarked unit. The presail conference is an essential part of the compatibility analysis, as it provides key personnel of the participating units with a formal forum to address the concept of upcoming operations at sea as well as procedural and safety issues. A presail conference should be scheduled to solidify all planning and coordination conducted to date, resolve outstanding issues or operational challenges, and confirm embarkation planning. Most integration issues are listed in the embarked unit pre-deployment planning checklist. (Annex B, "Embarked Unit Pre-Deployment Planning Checklist," to Appendix C, "Pre-Deployment Planning Checklists"). Additionally, Navy pre-deployment planning issues are discussed in:

(1) NAVAIR 00-80T-122, *Helicopter Operating Procedures for Air-Capable Ships NATOPS Manual.*

(2) Commander, Naval Surface Forces Instruction 3500.4/Commander, Naval Air Atlantic Instruction 3500.51/Commander, Marine Forces Atlantic Order 3500.2, *Readiness Milestones for Amphibious Ships and Embarked Aviation Units.*

(3) LHA/LHD/mine countermeasure support NAVAIR 00-80T-106, *LHA/LHD NATOPS Manual.*

c. The presail conference is a formal visit to the ship by key personnel representing the embarking unit's maintenance, logistics and operations departments. The presail conference is necessary to discuss embarkation, maintenance, operations, C2 to include command relationships, ordnance, communications system support, habitability, safety, etc. in regards to the upcoming deployment. Typically, when USA or United States Air Force (USAF) units embark aboard ship the personnel of both the embarking unit and the ship have limited knowledge of each other's capabilities and operational concepts. Nothing should be assumed by either party when planning for helicopter and tiltrotor aircraft operations. It is essential, starting with the presail conference and continuing throughout the planning process, that unit and ship personnel be detailed and meticulous utilizing the checklists and other references listed in this publication.

d. **Pre-Embarkation Unit Visit.** Prior to and/or following the presail conference, it is imperative that the embarking unit tour and become familiar with work spaces, living spaces, maintenance and storage areas, and support equipment available. Quite often, additional compatibility issues will arise when the operating spaces are actually visited by the embarking unit. This is when the space constraints inherent with shipboard operations become apparent to the embarking unit.

e. **Points of Contact (POCs).** A key element to successful presail visits is developing a POCs list. Figures II-1, II-2, and II-3 show general POCs aboard different ship types, their functions, responsibilities, and their embarking unit counterparts. Embarking unit personnel and ship counterparts should meet after the presail conference to exchange information on requirements/capabilities and coordinate onload and subsequent operations.

f. **Mission Integration.** The degree to which the operations of the embarked unit are merged or deconflicted from those of the ship is dependent on several factors, listed below.

(1) The unit with the priority mission will determine mission requirements; therefore, mission priorities may shift among several units as phases of an operation develop or are completed. The most likely mission integration scenarios occur in support of contingency operations. Probable scenarios include:

(a) Helicopter/tiltrotor aircraft units fly out to the ship. The ship sails to the mission area where the unit executes the mission and returns to the ship. The ship sails to the fly-off point and the units fly off to return to base.

(b) The ship provides a safe haven for helicopter/tiltrotor aircraft units based and operating ashore.

(c) The helicopter/tiltrotor aircraft units fly out to the ship after support personnel and troops embark in port. The ship provides transportation to the operational area and launches waves for an operation, then transports the helicopter/tiltrotor aircraft and aircrew personnel back to home base.

(2) When planning a long-term embarkation, the embarking unit's planner must then determine if organic ship aircraft will also be embarked. If no organic aircraft are embarked, then mission integration issues should be minimal.

(3) With organic air assets embarked, operational scenarios for different helicopter/tiltrotor aircraft compositions can be compared for fully integrated, semi-integrated, or coordinated flight operations. Flight operations are considered fully integrated when non-naval helicopter/tiltrotor aircraft launches and recoveries are accomplished during regular cyclic fixed-wing flight operations for aircraft carriers, or during regular flight operations for other class ships. Semi-integrated operations describe conditions where naval aircraft and helicopters/tiltrotor aircraft operate in sequential periods. Coordinated flight operations refer to the case where helicopter/tiltrotor aircraft operations take place in a single period outside scheduled naval flight operations for the CVW, ACE, or ACS.

## Planning Points of Contact on Aircraft Carriers

| Navy | Responsibility | Army/Air Force Counterpart |
|---|---|---|
| Commanding Officer (CO) | Responsible for mission execution/ accomplishment and safe rotocraft operations. | Commander |
| Executive Officer | Responsible to CO for mission execution and coordination between shipboard departments. Oversees administration and embarkation details. | S-1/G-1/A-1, Director of Operations |
| Strike Operations Officer | Schedules mission and training evolutions; flight planning and scheduling. | S-3/G-3/A-3 |
| Air Officer | Flight deck and flight operations. | S-3/G-3/A-3 |
| Flight Deck Control | Aircraft movement to accommodate maintenance, ordnance upload, and prelaunch positioning on the flight deck. | Aviation Maintenance Officer |
| Hangar Deck Control | Aircraft movement to accommodate maintenance on the hangar deck. | Aviation Maintenance Officer |
| Supply Officer | Hotel services, parts/material replenishment. | S-4/G-4/A-4 |
| First Lieutenant | Loading and unloading cargo. | S-4/G-4/A-4 |
| Weapons Officer | Controls ordnance on/off load, buildup, strikedown, issue, and accounting. | S-3/G-3/A-3 |
| Communications Officer | Communications capabilities and requirements, and coordination. | S-6/A-6 |
| Electronic Warfare Officer | Electronic missions, detection and counter-detection. | S-3/G-3/A-3 |
| Aircraft Intermediate Maintenance Department | Intermediate level maintenance assistance for engine, hydraulic, and electronic component repairs. | Aviation Maintenance Officer |
| Chief Engineer | Responsible for main propulsion (except on aircraft carrier, nuclear) electrical power, fuel, water production, and fire fighting systems. | S-4/G-4/A-4 |
| Combat Information Center Officer | Coordinates intelligence resources, requirements, briefings, debriefings; conducts mission briefs and mission debriefs. | S-2/G-2/A-2 |

NOTE:
When the carrier air wing (CVW) is embarked the air wing commander (CAG) may be designated to coordinate embarkation efforts for both Navy squadrons and embarking Army and Air Force units. The point of contact will be the CAG embark officer. When CVW is not embarked, the air boss or the ship's 1st Lieutenant may be tasked with coordination. Either way the embarking unit(s) will need to coordinate closely with both.

**Figure II-1. Planning Points of Contact on Aircraft Carriers**

## Planning Points of Contact on Amphibious Aviation Assault Ships

| Navy | Responsibility | Army/Air Force Counterpart |
|---|---|---|
| Commanding Officer (CO) | Responsible for mission execution/accomplishment and safe rotocraft operations. | Commander |
| Executive Officer | Responsible to CO for mission execution and coordination between shipboard departments. Oversees administration and embarkation details. | S-1/G-1/A-1, Director of Operations |
| Combat Cargo Officer | Embark coordination. | Unit Embark Officer |
| Operations Officer | Schedules missions and training evolutions. Flight planning and scheduling. | S-3/G-3/A-3 |
| Air Officer | Flight deck and flight operations. | S-3/G-3/A-3 |
| Aircraft Intermediate Maintenance Department | Intermediate level maintenance assistance for engine, hydraulic, and electronic component repairs. | Aviation Maintenance Officer |
| Flight Deck Control | Aircraft movement to accommodate maintenance, ordnance upload, and prelaunch positioning on the flight deck. | Aviation Maintenance Officer |
| Hangar Deck Control | Aircraft movement to accommodate maintenance on the hangar deck. | Aviation Maintenance Officer |
| Supply Officer | Hotel services, parts/material replenishment. | S-4/G-4/A-4 |
| First Lieutenant | Loading and unloading cargo. | S-4/G-4/A-4 |
| Weapons Officer | Controls ordnance on/off load, buildup, strikedown, issue, and accounting. | S-3/G-3/A-3 |
| Communications Officer | Communications capabilities and requirements, and coordination. | S-6/A-6 |
| Electronic Warfare Officer | Electronic missions, detection and counter-detection. | S-3/G-3/A-3 |
| Chief Engineer | Responsible for main propulsion, electrical power, fuel, water production, and maintenance of fire fighting systems. | S-4/G-4/A-4 |
| Combat Information Center Officer | Coordinates intelligence resources, requirements, briefings, debriefings; conducts mission briefs and mission debriefs. | S-2/G-2/A-2 |

**Figure II-2. Planning Points of Contact on Amphibious Aviation Assault Ships**

(a) **Fully Integrated Flight Operations.** These operations are the most difficult to coordinate, conduct, and sustain but can provide the best opportunities for mission integration and allow helicopters/tiltrotor aircraft to take advantage of carrier strike group direct-support capabilities. Fully integrated flight operations from ARG ships can take advantage of integral ARG/Marine expeditionary unit capabilities. Fully integrated

## Planning Points of Contact on Air-Capable Ships

| Navy | Responsibility | Army/Air Force Counterpart |
|---|---|---|
| Commanding Officer (CO) | Responsible for mission execution/accomplishment and safe rotocraft operations. | Commander |
| Executive Officer | Responsible to CO for mission execution and coordination between shipboard departments. Oversees administration and embarkation details. | S-1/G-1/A-1, Director of Operations |
| Operations Officer | Schedules missions and training evolutions. Flight planning and scheduling. | S-3/G-3/A-3 |
| Supply Officer | Hotel services, parts/material replenishment. | S-4/G-4/A-4 |
| First Lieutenant | Responsible for the maintenance of the flight deck and training of flight deck personnel. | S-4/G-4/A-4 |
| Helicopter Control Officer | Coordinates flight deck and flight operations. | S-3/G-3/A-3 |
| Weapons Officer | Controls ordnance on/off load, buildup, strikedown, issue, and accounting. | S-3/G-3/A-3 |
| Communications Officer | Communications capabilities and requirements, and coordination. | S-6/A-6 |
| Electronic Warfare Officer | Electronic missions, detection and counter-detection. | S-3/G-3/A-3 |
| Chief Engineer | Responsible for main propulsion, electrical power, fuel, water production, and maintenance of fire fighting systems. | S-4/G-4/A-4 |
| Combat Information Center Officer | Coordinates intelligence resources, requirements, briefings, debriefings; conducts mission briefs and mission debriefs. | S-2/G-2/A-2 |

**Figure II-3. Planning Points of Contact on Air-Capable Ships**

flight operations have few advantages for cruiser-destroyer class ships because of the limited deck and hangar space.

1. **Aircraft Carrier Operations.** Fully integrated flight operations aboard aircraft carriers are difficult under optimal conditions and become more so under adverse conditions. If fully integrated flight operations are contemplated, then a reduction in air wing composition must also be considered.

2. **Amphibious Aviation Assault Ship.** Integrating helicopter/tiltrotor aircraft units into the ARG mission may be achieved in several ways. Depending on the unit size and composition, it may be possible for the embarked unit to operate from the smaller decks in the ARG. If unit size or composition makes this difficult, some helicopter/tiltrotor aircraft assets may be detached to other ships in the ARG to make room aboard the AAS.

<u>3.</u> **ACS Operations.** ACSs typically carry a detachment of one or two organic helicopters/tiltrotor aircraft. Not all of these ships provide hangar facilities or mechanical handling equipment. Helicopters have operated safely and successfully from ACSs, but at some cost to traditional maritime missions. Embarkation of helicopters/tiltrotor aircraft for short periods may require a ship's organic helicopters to temporarily operate from other locations, potentially impacting that ship's mission. If integrated fueling/arming operations can be accomplished while organic assets are airborne or hangared, the mission impact can be minimized.

(b) **Semi-Integrated Flight Operations.** Inserting a flight period (cycle) dedicated to helicopter/tiltrotor aircraft operations between scheduled naval flight operation periods (cycles) combines some of the advantages of coordinated operations while removing some of the operational difficulty and risk of fully integrated flight operations.

(c) **Coordinated Flight Operations.** Although easier to schedule and coordinate, coordinated (nonsimultaneous) fixed tiltrotor aircraft and rotary wing operations have certain disadvantages. Non-naval flight operations take place during what would normally be nonflying hours. This can overwork the ship's air department personnel, significantly impact aircraft respotting, and hinder flight deck maintenance required to enable the next day's flight operations.

g. **Ordnance Planning.** Detailed presail/pre-embarkation planning for ordnance is even more important in the joint environment when individual Service processes/procedures may differ. If all or a portion of the ship's mission/cargo ammunition must be off-loaded to accommodate required helicopter, tiltrotor aircraft, or infantry ammunition, significant advanced planning will be required. Ordnance planning for helicopter and tiltrotor operations involves significant, in-depth research on the type of ordnance to be embarked aboard ship, including assuring WSESRB/Navy Ordnance Safety and Security Activity (NOSSA) approval of the ordnance identified for shipboard loadout and employment, WSESRB approved ordnance containers for shipboard operations, and the test data for ordnance designed with EIDs to determine shipboard HERO susceptibility.

(1) Non-Navy ordnance aboard ships is one of the most critical helicopter and tiltrotor operations issues and must be addressed early in pre-deployment planning. Direct liaison between the embarking unit's ordnance officer and the ship's weapons department representatives will identify and/or solve many of the associated compatibility, procedural, and training issues. Initial planning for the onload of non-Navy ordnance aboard a ship may require close coordination with the NOSSA located in Indian Head, Maryland, (http://www.nossa.navsea.navy.mil). The Web site provides information on ordnance physical security, insensitive munitions, and ordnance safety aboard Navy ships. NOSSA will be the POC for joint ordnance compatibility waivers. This ordnance information will assist the embarking unit when preparing for shipboard helicopter operations involving non-Navy ordnance. NAVSEA OP 4, *Ammunition and Explosives Safety Afloat,* is a comprehensive Navy directive delineating ordnance handling and storage procedures aboard Navy ships (http://navsea.navy.mil). Infantry ordnance is not common to most ship's

magazines. Planners should research all available data thoroughly before the presail conference.

(2) If the assigned ship and embarked helicopter detachment are not deployed, a pre-embarkation ordnance planning conference will be scheduled by the appropriate geographic combatant commander (GCC), preferably at least six months prior to the planned sail date, with all participating, to identify the support required and the timelines/responsibilities to put that support in place. The T/M/S of aircraft, including the installed aircraft weapons control systems and the ordnance weapon systems planned for shipboard employment require NOSSA CO approval prior to ammunition/explosives (A/E) onload. Required ordnance data is identified below. This data is also required for HERO EMCON considerations. NOSSA approved USA ordnance is identified in NAVSEA SW020-AC-SAF-010, *Transportation and Storage Data for Ammunition, Explosives, and Related Hazardous Materials,* where required packaging and explosive stowage data are included for each ordnance by NSN. Requests for A/E that are not included in NAVSEA SW020-AC-SAF-010 shall be referred by the ship to the type commander (TYCOM) and NOSSA for resolution. Deviation from the explosive safety standards set forth in NAVSEA OP 4, *Ammunition and Explosives Safety Afloat,* requires a waiver to be submitted by the host ship with supporting rationale from the affected GCC.

(3) **Defense Message Handling System (DMHS).** The ordnance onload requires extensive preplanning and coordination by ship's force. Chief of Naval Operations (CNO) approved waivers may be required for pierside loading, depending on the area and location. To ensure the onload is conducted smoothly and efficiently, it is imperative that the ordnance depot or ammunition stock point keep the ship and the helicopter/tiltrotor aircraft detachment constantly up to date on the types and quantities of ordnance to be loaded/employed via DMHS in the following format:

(a) **NALC or DODIC.**

(b) **NSN.** An NSN will be used for locating detailed information on each item.

(c) **Quantity.** Total quantity of each NALC/DODIC.

(d) **Lot Number.** The ammunition lot number (ALN) or serial number (SN) when available. Refer to Naval Supply Systems Command (NAVSUP) Publication (P)-724, *Conventional Ordnance Stockpile Management/*P-801, *Notice of Ammunition Reclassification (NAR) Manual* and P-802, *Navy Ammunition Logistics Codes,* for details on mandatory identification and control requirements.

(e) **Hazard Classification.** Used to determine the stowage compatibility/segregation for A/E. Verification through NAVSEA SW020-AC-SAF-010 is mandatory.

(f) **Container Identification and Dimensions.** If at all possible, information on the dimensions of the A/E containers separately and as palletized unit loads should be provided to ensure adequate stowage space is available aboard the ship. Verification through NAVSEA SW020-AC-SAF-010 is mandatory.

(g) **Number of Palletized Lifts.** Required for pierside crane services and for onload evolution timing.

(h) **Applicable NAR.** All United States Navy (USN) ammunition and most USA A/E are catalogued in the Ordnance Information System. When an item of A/E by ALN or SN requires a change in the material condition code of a DODIC/NALC lot or SN, a NAR is promulgated by Naval Operational Logistics Support Center (NOLSC). A similar control system is in place for USA A/E. To ensure that ship's supporting special operations forces (SOF) units are continually aware of any change in the materiel condition of embarked SOF A/E, NOLSC includes USA ammunition reclassification in Navy NARs. To ensure there is no oversight or omission in the USN NAR, the appropriate GCC shall ensure the supporting Army ammunition supply point (ASP) is provided the DMHS plain language address directory (PLAD) of the host ship. The ASP shall provide the host ship with all related USA A/E material condition reclassification action on a continuing basis until the SOF and USA A/E is completely expended or off-loaded.

(i) **Small Arms Weapons.** A list of all small arms weapons, by type and quantity, being deployed aboard the ship is required to ensure secure stowage requirements are available.

h. **Administration**

(1) The ship's XO is responsible for all administrative matters aboard ship. The XO coordinates the ship's staff and ensures that the ship functions as a team. The XO holds daily department head meetings, normally in the evening, to discuss the next day's schedule. A senior officer from the embarked unit should attend these department head meetings to coordinate the ship's schedule with the unit's operations, training, and other needs.

(2) The ship's administrative department handles routine administrative issues supporting Navy personnel. Regulations provide the ship's CO authority to hold Article 15 proceedings over all personnel onboard their ship regardless of Service branch. The ship's CO may defer this authority to the senior officer of the embarking unit. Potential good order and discipline procedures should be discussed prior to embarkation.

(3) The embarking unit should confirm whether the ship has migrated to the cashless, debit-card based Navy Cash system for messing and ships store purchases (to include vending machines).

i. **C2 Planning**

(1) Available space, types, and availability of equipment aboard the ship govern C2 planning considerations. Space constraints may require the embarked unit(s) to be divided and placed on more than one ship, further exacerbating the challenges. Command and staff action and control of non-naval embarked units may require modifications to unit SOPs (both ship and embarked unit). Basic communications, detailed planning, rehearsals, and mission execution are all more difficult whether forces are located on one ship or on several ships.

(2) Ships are designed and built to perform a specific set of missions. Accordingly, under most circumstances, a ship's CO will be required to fulfill the assigned missions in addition to providing support to an assigned embarked unit. Most ships are not designed to facilitate the normal operations and mission accomplishment of embarked units, especially in terms of communications systems and intelligence support. It is critical that leaders fully understand the capabilities, limitations, and needs of all forces (ships and embarked units) and develop a plan that will satisfy overall mission accomplishment. The following are typical planning tasks:

(a) Establish clear command relationship and authorities for all organizations aboard each ship.

(b) Ensure designation of a senior officer for oversight of embarked units.

(c) Determine who is responsible for specific functions/coordination.

(d) Determine working space and communications requirements for embarked units.

(e) Determine areas where it is advantageous for ship's company and embarked units to work collectively.

(f) Establish air control tower manning requirements: primary flight control (PRIFLY)/helicopter control officer (HCO).

(g) Establish intelligence center manning requirements.

(h) Establish communications center manning requirements.

(i) Establish strike operations/combat information center/HDC/AATCC manning requirements.

(j) Determine onload and/or off-load locations for ordnance.

(k) Determine EMCON procedures.

(l) Determine required/available/assigned frequencies.

(m) Determine communications systems material security requirements.

(n) Determine potential RF interference.

(o) Determine embarked unit's communications requirements and employment procedures.

(p) Determine EMV to aircraft.

(q) Establish procedures for HERO.

j. **Operations.** The operations section supports mission planning which is conducted backwards from the time on target at the objective. It should include the following considerations at a minimum:

(1) C2.

(2) Control measures.

(3) Controlling agencies.

(4) Number of helicopters/tiltrotors per wave/serial.

(5) Number of waves/serial.

(6) Time sequence (briefs, preflights, spotting, takeoff, rendezvous, en route, etc.).

(7) Helicopter/tiltrotor spotting for launch.

(8) Unit training.

(9) Daily scheduling.

(10) Ship's POD.

(11) Air tasking order or air plan/load plan.

(12) En route planning (ship to the objective).

(13) Debarkation planning (moving helicopter/tiltrotor aircraft, troops, and equipment ashore) to support the mission. Coordination should be conducted if sling-load operations are envisioned.

k. **Medical.** Medical health services vary widely depending on the class of the ship. Single-spot ACSs may have only an independent duty corpsman and no dental services, while multispot ACSs may have a physician and/or a dentist assigned. AASs and aircraft carriers usually have forward resuscitative care capability. Embarked unit planning should address medical and dental personnel to augment the ship's medical teams.

l. **Logistics/Supply**

(1) Navy ships do not normally stock other Service-unique items in their supply inventory. In addition to the standard aircraft maintenance packup kits containing small parts, tools, and consumables, a helicopter/tiltrotors maintenance unit assigned shipboard missions should pre-stage essential parts, such as rotor blades and engines, aboard ship prior to deployment. Ship's supply officers (SUPPOs) should inquire of the embarking unit which items they may need and make arrangements to establish a logistics line to obtain those items. Embarking units should contact the ship and discuss unique requirements with the SUPPO early in the planning cycle.

(2) The Navy supply system generally operates in several stages. Ships are supported via airheads and beach detachments. The airhead is a central location for all parts going to a particular ship. Expediters at the airhead forward supplies to an appropriate beach detachment located within flying range of the ship. The beach detachment collects the supplies and loads them aboard aircraft flying to the ships. Helicopter/tiltrotors units that are embarked aboard ship for an extended period should tie into the Navy supply pipeline to get replacement parts and supplies from their parent organizations. Embarked units should coordinate with the ship's SUPPO to have a liaison at each of the logistics stops in the ship's supply train.

*For specific guidance concerning logistic support, refer to Chapter IV, "Sustainment."*

m. **Vertical Takeoff and Landing Unmanned Aircraft System (VTOL-UAS).** In conducting VTOL-UAS operations, deconfliction with manned aircraft becomes the greatest issue to resolve. The VTOL-UAS will be required to operate under positive control and comply with published approach or departure procedures. In addition, significant effort and lead time may be required to support the installation of unmanned aircraft system (UAS) antennas, ground control station(s), and autonomous landing capability (such as UAS common automatic recovery system) aboard a ship. Additional considerations include:

(1) Reliable access to the EM spectrum;

(2) Frequency management; and

(3) Fuel supply storage.

*For further information on UAS planning considerations, refer to Field Manual (FM) 3-04.15, Navy Tactics, Techniques, and Procedures (NTTP) 3-55.14, Air Force Tactics, Techniques, and Procedures (Instruction) (AFTTP[I]) 3-2.64, Multi-Service Tactics, Techniques, and Procedures for Tactical Employment of Unmanned Aircraft Systems.*

## 4. Pre-Deployment Training and Certification

a. **General Training Requirements.** The training requirements in this chapter will be met except for immediate operational requirements where the success of the mission would be clearly jeopardized by delaying operations until required training can be obtained. These requirements include qualification training as well as unit certification that fall into two general categories:

(1) **Pre-Embarkation Training**

(a) Shipboard and aircraft fire fighting training.

(b) Aviation ordnance training and follow-on qualifications/certifications.

(c) Aircrew qualification and currency.

(2) **Embarkation Training.** This training is conducted by the ship's company indoctrination organization. It should include the following: shipboard electrical safety; storage, handling, and disposal of hazardous or flammable material; hearing conservation; emergency escape breathing device and oxygen breathing apparatus; HERO and EMCON plans; material conditions of readiness; basic damage control organization and embarked aviation detachment responsibilities; abandon ship bill/life raft stations; emergency egress blindfold drill (berthing compartment and workspace); ship's battle bill and man overboard bill; and GQ (with and without flight quarters).

b. **Detachment Ground Personnel Training.** Maintenance personnel and aircrew assigned to helicopter/tiltrotor aircraft detachments that maintain a capability to operate from ships will receive joint helicopter operations orientation training in order to ensure their safety and effectiveness at sea. These requirements apply to embarked operations and are not intended to restrict personnel whose exposure to the shipboard environment is limited to DLQ training periods.

c. **Aircrew Training, Qualification, and Currency Requirements.** Pilots obtain initial, recurrent, and requalification training for type aircraft in accordance with (IAW) parent Service directives as appropriate. The DLQ identified in Figure II-4 are derived directly from the January 2002, Memorandum of Understanding (MOU), *Army/Air Force Deck Landing Qualification*, between the Department of the Navy (DON) and the Departments of the Army and the Air Force.

d. **Certification.** Before embarkation, helicopter/tiltrotor aircraft detachments will be certified for shipboard operations by their unit commander or other authority. This certification will ensure that training requirements set forth in this publication have been met and that the detachment has met parent Service training requirements for the intended mission. Any specific training shortfalls or additional training intended after embarkation should be briefed during the presail conference when applicable and appropriate.

## United States Army/United States Air Force Deck Landing Requirements for One-spot Ships and Multispot Ships

| Requirements | | | Day (D) | Night Unaided (N) | Night Aided (NVD) |
|---|---|---|---|---|---|
| Initial Qualification | Instructor | | DLQ current IP or USN/USMC HAC | N DLQ current IP or USN/USMC HAC | NVD DLQ current IP or USN/USMC HAC |
| | Prerequisite | | Qualified in the aircraft, DLQ academics | Day DLQ current, 2 ship or simulator DLQs (D/N/NVD) within 7 Days | Day DLQ current, 2 ship or simulator DLQs (D/N/NVD) within 14 Days |
| | FDLPs | Within 14 days | 5 FDLPs in aircraft or qualified simulator | 5 Night unaided FDLPs in aircraft or qualified simulator | 5 NVD FDLPs in aircraft or qualified simulator |
| | DLQs | | 5 | 5 | 5 |
| | Period | | 6 Months (1SS), 1 Year (MSS) | | |
| Currency | DLQs | | 5 DLQs (D/N/NVD) within: 6 months (1SS), 1 year (MSS) | 5 N DLQs (D/N/NVD) within: 6 months (1SS), 1 year (MSS) | 5 NVD DLQs within: 6 months (1SS), 1 year (MSS) |
| | Night DLQ Prerequisite | | N/A | 2 ship or simulator DLQs (D/N/NVD) within 7 days | 2 ship or simulator DLQs (D/N/NVD) within 14 days or 2 ship or simulator NVD DLQs within 45 days |
| Simulator DLQ Currency | Instructor | | DLQ Current IP/simulator IP or USN/USMC HAC | N DLQ Current IP/simulator IP or USN/USMC HAC | NVD DLQ Current IP/simulator IP or USN/USMC HAC |
| | Simulator DLQs | | 5 DLQs (D/N/NVD) | 5 N DLQs | 5 NVD DLQs |
| | Prerequisite | | Day DLQ current | Night DLQ current | NVD DLQ current |
| | Period | | (1SS) 6 months from simulator flight, not to exceed 1 year from last 1SS landing. (MSS) 1 year from simulator flight, not to exceed 2 years from last MSS landing. | | |
| DLQ Academics | | | Required for all initial DLQ training, or if currency has elapsed for both 1SSs and MSSs. | | |

Legend

| | | | | |
|---|---|---|---|---|
| 1SS | one-spot ship | | MSS | multispot ship |
| DLQ | deck landing qualification | | N/A | not applicable |
| FDLP | flight deck landing practice | | USMC | United States Marines Corps |
| HAC | helicopter aircraft commander | | USN | United States Navy |
| IP | instructor pilot | | | |

**Figure II-4. United States Army/United States Air Force Deck Landing Requirements for One-Spot Ships and Multispot Ships**

Certification is not required for all training operations that do not require embarkation (e.g., DLQ). In addition, all personnel assigned duties involving the handling of A/E shall be qualified and certified for the task IAW Chief of Naval Operations Instruction (OPNAVINST) 8023.24, *Navy Personnel Ammunition and Explosive Handling Qualification and Certification Program,* and NAVSEA OP 4, *Ammunition and Explosives Safety Afloat.* This will be accomplished by the unit commander providing the ship with documentation that aviation ordnance device-handling personnel have been thoroughly trained, qualified, and certified on the safe and efficient handling of aviation ordnance.

e. **Helicopter/Tiltrotor Aircraft Specifications.** Prior to operations, and when requested, the detachment OIC will make available diagrams of embarked aircraft to the HCO or air officer (air boss) and crash and salvage parties.

f. Requirements for aviation detachment personnel assigned to flight deck duties:

(1) Aviators should be current and qualified to fly before participation in shipboard operations.

(2) Shipboard fire fighting indoctrination training is required for flight deck personnel.

5. **Embarkation Planning**

a. **General.** Embarkation planning involves reverse planning from the objective, to the landing zone, to the ship, and to the port of embarkation (POE) such that the equipment that will be needed first is the last equipment loaded onboard ship. Successful embarkation plan development requires early coordination between the embarking unit and the ship's crew. Both should work concurrently on developing embarkation milestones, scheduling an embarkation conference, staffing advance parties (to include ship guides), assigning embarkation coordinators, and developing a load plan. Most of the issues concerning embarkation should be discussed during the embarkation and presail conferences. See Appendix C, "Pre-Deployment Planning Checklists."

b. **Embarkation Procedures/Coordination.** The embarkation process will be enhanced by assigning single POCs for both the ship and the embarking unit. It is imperative that the unit and ship embarkation coordinators work together to develop embarkation milestones. Once the milestones are published, changes must be coordinated through both the unit and the ship.

(1) Embarkation planning issues to be discussed include:

(a) Embarkation team organization for each Service unit.

(b) Personnel requirements.

(c) Communications (means of communication during the evolution and identification of those personnel who should be communicating).

(d) Materials handling equipment (MHE).

(e) Safety.

(f) Cargo handling systems.

(g) Securing of cargo and vehicles.

(h) Traffic routes for cargo and personnel moving on and off the ship.

(i) Onload and/or off-load points.

(j) Types and amounts of cargo, ordnance, and vehicles.

(k) Operational checks of MHE prior to onload and off-load.

(l) Coordinating communications security storage requirements and agreements.

(2) Successful embarkation plan development requires early coordination between the embarking unit and the ship's crew. Both should work together to develop embarkation milestones, scheduling an embarkation conference, staffing advance parties (to include ship guides), assigning embarkation coordinators, and developing a load plan.

c. Joint guidance for embarkation is provided in Joint Publication (JP) 3-02.1, *Amphibious Embarkation and Debarkation.* The Navy/Marine Corps follow embarkation guidelines outlined in Marine Corps Reference Publication (MCRP) 4-11.3G, *Unit Embarkation Handbook.* General guidelines for embarkation can be found in OPNAVINST 5720.2, *Embarkation of US Naval Ships.*

d. Naval personnel load cargo based on cube and weight. Any cargo that is not hand carried must be palletized and banded or loaded in standard International Organization for Standardization (ISO) configured equipment and containers (military van, container express, quadruple container, six-compartment container). When palletizing cargo, embarking units should plan on using one of the more commonly used sizes in North America (48" × 48", 48" × 40" or 42" × 42"). 463L pallets cannot be used unless arrangements can be made to provide Army low-profile forklifts on CVNs or AASs (Navy forklifts cannot handle 463L pallets). Failure to follow these simple palletizing requirements can delay embarkation and place both the ship and unit at risk. It is important to let the load officer know the volume and weight of crates and equipment containers so they can arrange the appropriate storage space on ship. In addition, they will need to know which items are necessary for ready access and which will be infrequent access/use items. A critical part of embarkation planning is the embarkation conference. This conference should be scheduled six months or more in advance or as early as possible in the planning process and shall address:

(1) Ordnance embarkation and ammunition reporting requirements.

(2) Load plan preparation and submission requirements.

(3) ISO container loading policy, constraints, and criteria.

(4) Naval support element lift footprint and assignment to ships.

(5) POE inspection requirements.

(6) Motor gasoline storage capacities, retrograde capabilities, and safety considerations.

(7) Aviation GSE embarkation requirements.

(8) Embarking unit accommodations, inspection timeline, reporting requirements, and methodology.

(9) US Customs and Department of Agriculture requirements.

(10) Embarkation schedule of events development, submission, and modifications.

(11) In-port loading of embarking unit personnel, supplies, and equipment.

(12) Compilation and distribution of command POCs.

(13) Munitions cross-decking and retrograde policy development.

(14) Hazardous materials (HAZMAT) (lithium batteries, sulfuric acid, calcium hypochlorite, etc.).

e. **Administrative/Training Coordination.** Shipboard operations are a complex orchestration of activities. Ship activities are planned during the ship's "8 o'clock reports" and planning board for training. The embarked unit should send a representative to each of these meetings. "8 o'clock reports" generally occur before 2000 hours (shipboard time). "8 o'clock reports" are scheduled and conducted by the ship's XO to collect status reports from the ship's department heads and coordinate and disseminate the next day's schedule.

f. Future events are discussed and scheduled during the planning board for training. This is the forum where the embarked unit will address unit-training requirements and coordinate and schedule these requirements with the various ships' departments whose services or spaces may be needed. Ship departments have periodic training requirements such as engineering casualty drills, and EMCON or deceptive lighting evolutions that may significantly impact the embarked unit's maintenance or flight operations. The planning board for training is the venue where these competing requirements are negotiated.

g. **Habitability Coordination.** Habitability issues should be coordinated with the designated ship's representative. Among the issues to coordinate are cleaning and preservation of embarked unit spaces and billeting and messing of embarked personnel.

h. **Embarked Unit Ship Support Requirements**

(1) **Information for Embarked Units.** Navy ships employ the team concept underway. Everyone aboard ship contributes to the success of the ship's mission and participates in policing the ship's common use areas. This generally involves temporary assignment of embarked personnel to the ship's supply department to augment ship's company personnel providing necessary services such as laundry, food preparation, and cleaning details. Embarking units must include this requirement in their overall plan by identifying personnel for these details (possibly from their support units).

(2) **Information for Ship's Personnel.** Embarking units are generally manned only for flying assigned missions. They are not manned to accommodate requests to augment ship's company in mess duties or working parties. In practice they are supported by other organizations that are specialized for specific support roles: field kitchen, quartermaster, security police, and maintenance units. Addressing augmentation requirements during the embarkation and presail conferences will allow the embarking unit to plan/arrange for personnel augmentation accommodation.

i. **Safety.** Embarking units will find the shipboard environment is like an industrial area. Ships are a collection of electrical, electronic, and mechanical equipment. HAZMAT storage/issue spaces are found in various locations dependent on ship class or type. Temporary HAZMAT storage lockers are located throughout the ship in spaces requiring frequent access to HAZMAT in performing daily routine tasks. Awareness of ship hazards and their locations is the first step toward safety aboard ship. Much of this information will be presented during shipboard indoctrination conducted by the ship's safety department after unit embarkation.

j. **General Onload.** There are several avenues for onload of personnel and equipment. For small units, embarking for short duration, flying everything aboard may be the preferred method. For larger units or for longer durations, a combination of pierside loading and fly-on may be the optimal method. Embarking units should have an advance party embark 48 to 96 hours prior to loading. This provides sufficient time to become familiar with the ship and establish coordination before cargo, vehicles, and personnel arrive. The advance party should be composed of personnel to coordinate all general onload preparation.

k. **Ordnance Onload.** Ordnance can be loaded pierside or flown aboard the ship while underway as cargo. Underway replenishment (connected/vertical) is prohibited for non-Navy packaged munitions due to safety considerations. After the supporting ordnance is identified per NAVSEA OP 4, *Ammunition and Explosives Safety Afloat,* and the operational commander identifies an onload target date to both the Service depot/ASP and the ship's weapons officer, the ship can arrange for onload through the applicable TYCOM. Similar arrangements will be made for the ordnance off-load following completion of the operational tasking. Full justification for any related waivers that must be submitted by the host ship will be provided by the embarking unit commander.

l. **Helicopter/Tiltrotor Aircraft Onload/Fly-On.** Coordination of fly-on from a shore site to a ship at sea will depend on distance between the ship and shore, available navigation aids, and communications between shore ATC and the ship's controllers. Several items should be coordinated and agreed upon before flying out to the ship (e.g., arrival sequence, ship's position, navigational aids [NAVAIDS]). Preferably, these items will be addressed and resolved not later than the presail conference.

## 6. Debarkation Planning

This section will cover some of the debarkation considerations. It is not an all-encompassing source document. This data forms the baseline from which ship and embarked unit personnel can begin to develop a debarkation plan. There are two debarkation processes to discuss. Mission debarkation is leaving the ship to conduct the mission (return to the ship is anticipated and expected) and is focused on operational concerns and support requirements. Post-mission debarkation is leaving the ship (return not anticipated). Post-mission debarkation is a mirror image of the embarkation process. Coordination for debarkation should begin well before the anticipated debarkation date. Discuss timelines and support requirements both on the ship and on shore. All areas covered in the embarkation conference should be addressed in debarkation planning.

a. **Mission Debarkation Procedures and Coordination.** Mission debarkation involves much of the ship and the embarked unit. Debarkation will proceed more smoothly with planning and close coordination among embarked units and the ship. Essential elements of mission debarkation are milestones, load planning, shipboard coordination, and staging.

b. **Post-Mission Debarkation Procedures and Coordination.** Like embarkation, assigning single POCs for both the ship and debarking unit will enhance the debarkation process. As soon as the anticipated debarkation date is estimated, debarkation coordinators should begin debarkation planning. The unit and ship debarkation coordinators should work together to develop debarkation milestones to provide a baseline for the debarkation evolution. The debarking unit and the ship should make every attempt to adhere to the published milestones. Once the milestones are published, changes must be coordinated through both the unit and the ship. Planning issues to consider include timeline; support requirements (shore, ship); ordnance and HAZMAT off-load; etc. Off-load will be most efficient if those responsible for moving the material off the ship are thoroughly familiar with the off-load plan. Prior to arriving pierside, the off-load coordinators should conduct a briefing for all involved personnel to cover the plan in detail.

c. **Helicopter/Tiltrotor Aircraft Off-Load/Fly-Off.** Embarked helicopter/tiltrotor aircraft may fly off the ship as it approaches port or in some cases may fly off the ship once it is pierside. When arranging to fly off, helicopter/tiltrotor aircraft units should ensure coordination among ATC (both ship and shore), the ship's operations and air departments, and unit shore personnel. Issues to consider prior to fly-off include departure sequence, ship's position, NAVAIDS, etc.

*For further information on debarkation planning, refer to JP 3-02.1, Amphibious Embarkation and Debarkation.*

7. **Safety**

    a. **Responsibility for Safety.** The CO of the ship has supervisory responsibility for the safety of embarked helicopters/tiltrotor aircraft at all times. The helicopter/tiltrotor aircraft unit CO or detachment OIC and the individual aircraft pilots are directly responsible for the safety of assigned aircraft and personnel. In questionable circumstances, the embarked unit CO or detachment OIC will make the final determination concerning flight safety of aircraft, crew, and passengers.

    b. **Risk Management.** Many embarking units are unfamiliar with the complexities and many hazards of the shipboard environment. Parent commands should provide embarking units with appropriate water survival aviation life support equipment and train them on the proper care and use during normal unit train-up. Awareness of ship hazards and their locations is the first step toward safety aboard ship. Much of this information will be presented during shipboard indoctrination conducted by the ship's safety department after unit embarkation. Items to discuss include:

    (1) Machinery noises and other routine shipboard activity, including night flight/amphibious operations, may affect crew rest.

    (2) The ship is an industrial environment. Shipboard electrical systems are different. Fire hazards present a greater risk aboard ship than in the field. Risk management depends heavily on awareness and avoidance of the hazards.

    (3) Hazardous chemicals, concentration of machinery, electronic emitters, and shipboard weapons stations compound the hazards.

    (4) Limited space and tight quarters present injury hazards from equipment and/or boxes hanging on the walls (bulkheads) and ceilings (overheads).

    (5) Shipboard drills require participation by all personnel aboard ship.

    (6) All embarked personnel should be aware of water survival techniques.

    (7) Personnel should be trained in the use of flight deck safety equipment.

    (8) Wind and ship motion may adversely impact what would otherwise be routine evolutions.

    (9) Shipboard activities must be coordinated to ensure incompatible evolutions do not occur in close proximity.

(10) Salt air exposure and its corrosive effects on airframe and electronic components/systems.

(11) Mitigation programs; tool control, foreign object damage (FOD) control, and shipwide drills.

(12) Shipboard standard terminology/compartment numbering.

c. **General Safety Measures.** The squadron CO or detachment OIC and ship personnel will evaluate the hazards involved in all phases of shipboard helicopter/tiltrotor aircraft operations and develop appropriate safety measures. Shipboard personnel will be trained in safe operating procedures before commencement of helicopter/tiltrotor aircraft operations.

(1) During flight operations, only those personnel whose presence is required will be allowed in the flight deck area. All other personnel will remain clear or below the flight deck.

(2) Personnel engaged in flight operations (other than aircrew member on participating aircraft) will wear approved head and ear protection, sound suppressors, safety goggles, steel-toe safety shoes, flotation devices, long-sleeved shirts or flight deck jerseys, and long trousers. Transient crews will wear appropriate clothing/equipment IAW parent Service directives. Reflective tape will be applied to headgear and/or the upper body area of flight deck personnel clothing or equipment. All personnel on exposed decks will remove their hats (except for approved fastened safety helmets) while helicopter/tiltrotor aircraft operations are being conducted. All personnel on the flight deck must be trained to take cover immediately on command of the flight deck officer, air officer, LSE, or landing signals officer (LSO).

(3) Personnel are allowed to transit the area under the rotor arc of an operating helicopter/tiltrotor aircraft only with the permission of the pilot (who will signal the LSE or LSO before permitting such passage). For operating helicopters configured with a tail rotor, persons transiting from one side to the other under the rotor arc will do so via the nose of the aircraft. The use of a guide to move personnel around turning aircraft rotor blades should be considered.

d. **Safety Concerns for Aircraft Passengers and Troop Movement.** All shipboard passenger transfers shall be conducted IAW OPNAVISNT 3710.7U, *NATOPS General Flight and Operating Instructions.* Ensure that passengers to be transferred are manifested and briefed per Service guidelines, NAVAIR 00-80T-105 CV NATOPS Manual, NAVAIR 00-80T-106 LHA/LHD NATOPS Manual, or NAVAIR 00-80T-122, *Helicopter Operating Procedures for Air-Capable Ships,* have proper cranial protection and emergency flotation devices, and have received a flight emergency briefing with a copy of the pertinent helicopter/tiltrotor aircraft emergency diagram.

e. **Safety Concerns for Transfer of Personnel by Hoist**

(1) If landing is not practicable, a transfer may be made by hoist. Passengers in the helicopter/tiltrotor aircraft will remain seated with safety belts secured at all times except when otherwise directed by a crewman during the actual hoist transfer. Personnel will be briefed on helicopter/tiltrotor aircraft ditching procedures and the proper position of the hoisting device. Personal baggage will not be carried during the hoisting operation.

(2) Flight deck personnel will ground out the helicopter/tiltrotor aircraft hoist cable prior to the passenger reaching the ship's deck.

(3) **Transfer of passengers by hoist at night is prohibited except in emergency situations.**

f. **Night Over-Water Helicopter/Tiltrotor Aircraft Passenger Flights.** Night over-water helicopter/tiltrotor aircraft passenger flights to/from carriers and/or amphibious ships are prohibited except in cases of operational necessity. Night helicopter/tiltrotor aircraft passenger flights to or from ACSs shall be limited to situations of an operational necessity to properly certified ships. These limitations do not preclude troop movement in support of amphibious, special warfare, and/or explosive ordnance disposal exercises/operations.

g. **General Flight Deck Hazards**

(1) **FOD.** All-weather deck areas, and particularly the flight deck, will be inspected before and monitored throughout all helicopter/tiltrotor aircraft operations to ensure that they are clear of FOD. FOD-producing material includes rags, paper, line, ball caps, hardware, and other matter that can be caught by air currents and damage aircraft or injure personnel.

(2) **Helicopter/Tiltrotor Aircraft Equipment Hazards.** Equipment aboard helicopters/tiltrotor aircraft can present unfamiliar dangers to ship personnel. Equipment restrictions and limitations should be discussed during the presail conference and reinforced during orientation.

(3) **Weapons Hazards**

(a) Helicopters/tiltrotor aircraft parked or operating in the vicinity of ship's weapons are subject to damage from rocket blast, gunfire concussion, and FOD from materials scattered when ship's weapons are fired. All appropriate measures should be taken to preclude the firing of any weapon in the vicinity of the helicopter/tiltrotor aircraft operating area when an aircraft is parked on deck or when flight operations are in progress. When weapons firing is anticipated, aircraft will be positioned outside the weapons blast or concussion range. If this is not possible, aircraft should be secured as far as is practical from the firing mounts, with doors and hatches open.

(b) Procedures for the custody and security of personal small arms (e.g., 9 millimeter and M4/M16 rifles) will be IAW the ship's current small arms (weapons) instruction and OPNAVINST 5530.13, *Department of the Navy Physical Security Instructions for Conventional Arms, Ammunition, and Explosives (AA&E)*.

h. **Emergency Procedures.** While aboard ship, there are generally two categories of emergencies: shipboard emergencies (especially shipwide emergencies) or aircraft emergencies. Each emergency situation is unique. Therefore, pre-established procedures may not hold in every instance, but the following general guidelines are appropriate:

(1) **Shipboard Emergencies and Drills.** These emergencies include "GQ" and "man overboard."

(a) GQ is a condition of readiness when naval action is imminent. All battle stations are fully manned and alert; ammunition is ready for instant loading; guns and guided missile launchers may be loaded. Normally, embarked personnel are directed to their working area or berthing area during GQ in order to allow ship's personnel to conduct battle or handle the emergency situation.

(b) "Man overboard" indicates there may be someone in the water who needs to be rescued. When "man overboard" is announced it is imperative that a visual muster be conducted of all personnel. An accurate muster is necessary to determine whether someone from the ship is, in fact, in the water, and who that person is. The muster report should be forwarded to damage control central or the bridge as required. The method for forwarding this information will depend on the ship's established procedures.

(2) **Aircraft Emergencies.** These emergencies fall into three basic categories: aircraft ditch or crash, an immediate landing, and a precautionary shipboard landing.

(a) Helicopter/tiltrotor aircraft emergency information will be passed to the flight deck crew and fire party either over the 1MC or the flight deck crew announcing system, whichever is most expedient.

(b) When the flight deck has an emergency and a crash alarm is sounded, unnecessary personnel will be cleared from the flight deck and surrounding area.

(c) During any emergency, the first consideration of the ship should be to close the distance to the helicopter/tiltrotor aircraft and prepare for immediate recovery. For single-spot ship emergencies, the senior member of the air detachment onboard the ship should report to the bridge. If the emergency involves a tail rotor malfunction, single engine condition, engine fire, or power loss, optimum relative wind for recovery is required. If a flight control malfunction is indicated, a stable flight deck with acceptable winds is warranted. Specific actions are outlined in aircraft flight manuals.

i. **Cold Weather Operations.** The operation of helicopters/tiltrotor aircraft in cold weather requires special procedures for maintenance, servicing, and operations. Extreme cold weather operations require advance preparations and special equipment and procedures. Allied Tactical Publication (ATP)-17, *Naval Arctic Manual,* is an excellent resource. It includes information on crew exposure, helicopter icing, and general cold weather operational guidance.

(1) **Environmental Considerations.** Adverse climatic and other environmental conditions at sea will affect ships and their equipment during cold weather operations.

(2) **Maintenance and Servicing.** While routine tasks take longer because of difficulties posed by low temperatures, aircraft and equipment can be maintained and serviced when exposed to temperatures as low as –40°Celsius (C). The time required to perform a maintenance task on an aircraft in cold weather is best determined by considering it to be a function of wind chill rather than temperature. Cold weather operation of helicopters/tiltrotor aircraft shall be IAW the applicable aircraft manual.

(3) When refueling at low temperatures, care should be taken because objects can become charged with static electricity more readily than at normal temperatures. Refueling should be carried out as soon as possible after shutdown to prevent water condensation inside fuel tanks.

(4) **Flight Operations.** All flight operations should be planned and scheduled with consideration for aircrew/passenger survival time and SAR capability in the area of operations. Personnel transfers to or from ships during cold weather operations should be kept to a minimum as required by operational necessity. Cold weather passenger transfers should be performed over the shortest distance possible, preferably within visual range. Transferring and receiving units should establish and maintain communications/radar contact for the duration of the transfer.

> *Arctic wind-chill factor near a hovering helicopter can freeze exposed flesh in a matter of seconds. Protective measures and frequent rotation of personnel should be considered.*

(5) **Cold-Water Estimated Survival Time.** Figure II-5 displays predicted cold-water survival time (defined as the time required to cool to –30°C) of lightly clothed, non-exercising humans in cold water. The graph shows a line for the average life expectancy and a broad zone that indicates the large amount of individual variability associated with different body size, build, fatness, physical fitness, and state of health. The zone would include approximately 95 percent of the variation expected for adult and teenage humans under the conditions specified. The zone would be shifted downward into the fast coolers section by physical activity (e.g., swimming) and upward into the slow coolers section for heavy clothing and/or protective behaviors (e.g., huddling with other survivors or adopting a fetal position in the water). Specialized insulated protective clothing (e.g., survival suits, wet suits) are capable of increasing survival time from 2 to 10 times (or more) the basic duration shown here. In the zone where death from hypothermia is highly improbable, cold water greatly facilitates death from drowning, often in the first 10 to 15 minutes, particularly for those not wearing flotation devices.

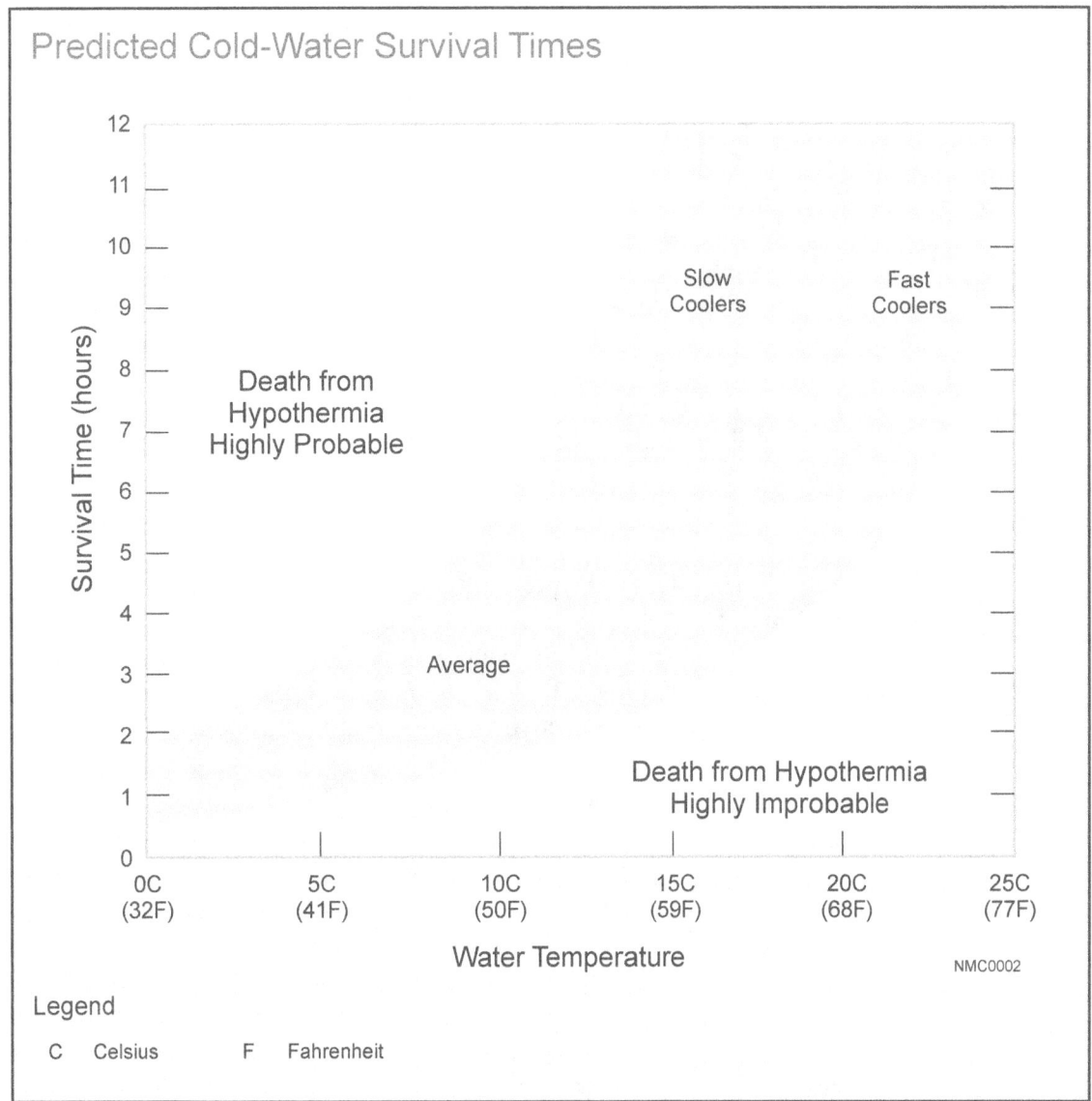

**Figure II-5. Predicted Cold-Water Survival Times**

## 8. Ordnance

a. **Ordnance Movement, Handling, and Stowage.** The movement, handling, and stowage of explosive ordnance carried aboard ships and aircraft is inherently dangerous. Shipboard handling/stowage of A/E is therefore governed by the most definitive and restrictive Department of Defense (DOD) regulations and precautions. What might be considered a relatively minor explosive incident ashore could be catastrophic underway due to the confined environment aboard ship. Safety is the responsibility of all levels of command, and understanding the risk is paramount. Sound knowledge and a healthy respect for ordnance operations will help ensure that safety requirements are met. Safety must not be jeopardized by either the introduction of weapons not approved for shipboard employment by WSESRB/CNO or use of inadequately trained personnel to accomplish explosive tasks. The destructive capacity of explosives has the potential to severely cripple or destroy the ship and crew in a matter of minutes. It is therefore imperative that mandatory safety procedures are complied with at all times by qualified and certified personnel with the appropriate supervision.

(1) **Ordnance Onload.** Ordnance onload requires extensive preplanning and coordination by ship's company. CNO approved waivers may be required. To ensure the onload is conducted smoothly and efficiently, it is imperative that the embarking helicopter/tiltrotor aircraft detachment keeps the ship's weapons department and safety personnel up-to-date on a continual basis regarding the types and quantities of ordnance to be loaded/employed. Message format will be used initially and when any change occurs. Per OPNAVINST 8023.24, *Navy Personnel Ammunition and Explosive Handling Qualification and Certification Program,* all personnel handling aviation ordnance, onboard Navy ships, will be fully trained and qualified and certified for all assigned tasks. The ship's explosive handling qualification and certification board qualify ship's personnel per this directive.

(2) **Embarked USA/USAF Helicopter/Tiltrotor Aircraft Detachment Aviation Ordnance Device Handling.** Safe aviation ordnance handling is critical to the survivability of the ship and the safety of all hands. The qualification and certification of personnel tasked with the safe and efficient handling of aviation ordnance is no more effective than the command certification of a thorough and effective training program that covers each.

9. **Electromagnetic Environmental Effects**

a. **Introduction.** Operations in and around ships subject both the helicopter/tiltrotor aircraft and the ship to E3 emissions neither may have been designed to encounter. When planning shipboard helicopter/tiltrotor operations, potential radiation hazards, EMI, and electronic vulnerability effects must be considered so that applicable transmitter conditions can be set prior to arrival of helicopters/tiltrotor aircraft aboard the ship. Planners should contact the Joint Spectrum Center (JSC) to receive proper HERO and EMV guidance prior to issuing authorization to conduct helicopter/tiltrotor aircraft operations.

b. Conducting flight operations on and around ships places a helicopter/tiltrotor aircraft in close proximity to dozens of high-powered transmitters, and can make them susceptible to E3. Among the primary areas of concern for the planner are the susceptibility of unshielded helicopter/tiltrotor aircraft electronic systems and non-maritime ordnance carried by helicopters/tiltrotor aircraft or personnel to shipboard emitters and the susceptibility of shipboard sensors and communications to helicopter/tiltrotor aircraft emitters. In a worst case scenario, these transmitters can detonate or dud ordnance, impact flight control systems, and permanently damage helicopter/tiltrotor aircraft avionics and electronics. Unlike their USN/United States Marine Corps (USMC) counterparts, most helicopters/tiltrotor aircraft were not designed to operate in the shipboard EME. And since many of these high-powered transmitters are utilized by the ship's air/missile defense, navigation and communications systems, they cannot be simply turned off when helicopters/tiltrotor aircraft are embarked. Therefore, many precautions must be taken to protect these aircraft from the E3 impact of the shipboard transmitters.

(1) The integrated joint force operational EME is continuously changing as existing systems are modified and new systems are installed. Joint operations increase the potential for safety, interoperability, and reliability problems if the platforms and their associated systems and equipment, including avionics, ordnance, and other embarked systems, are exposed to an operational EME different from those for which they were designed and tested. Integrated joint operations aboard ACSs require a careful balance of weapons, EMCON, delivery platforms, and ordnance handling procedures in the most extreme EMEs. The following sections present guidelines for several E3 issues which can adversely affect operations.

(2) **HERO**

(a) **Purpose.** A major concern when operating helicopters/tiltrotor aircraft on ships is HERO. This section covers the procedures and guidelines that are necessary for safe shipboard helicopter/tiltrotor operations from a HERO perspective.

(b) DOD and JSC work with NOSSA and Naval Surface Warfare Center Dahlgren Division (NSWCDD) to determine what safety measures are required to mitigate the risks associated with non-Navy ordnance aboard Navy ships. This analysis must be accomplished prior to embarking any non-Navy ordnance onboard ships. To ensure that this is accomplished quickly and efficiently, the embarked units must be prepared to provide a DODIC or NALC and a complete NSN list of all ordnance items that will be brought to the ship. This includes aircraft cartridge-actuated devices, fuel tank, fire suppression, aircraft ordnance, and personnel munitions.

(c) **Introduction.** Ordnance items containing electro-explosive devices (EEDs) are sensitive to EM energy from a variety of sources, such as radar and communication transmitters, including handheld walkie-talkie devices. Extreme caution must be exercised to ensure that EEDs are not exposed to an EME that would cause inadvertent activation of the ordnance, thus causing injury to personnel and/or damage to property. This potential hazard exists in all life cycle phases of an ordnance item, including storage, transportation, assembly, disassembly, handling, loading, staging, when platform loaded, and immediately post launch. There are numerous at-sea and in-the-air situations where an ordnance item may become exposed to an unacceptable level of EM energy. Ordnance items that contain EEDs can be inadvertently activated or dudded by the EM fields typically present in the exposed topside areas of operational ships. The operational restriction of transmitter emissions through the use of standard EMCON procedures may reduce vital sensory data needed for successful battle force management in a hostile environment. Any unnecessary restriction placed upon radar, communication, electronic warfare, and other shipboard systems to avoid ordnance mishaps can severely limit the host platform's warfighting capability. Accordingly, it becomes essential that comprehensive and accurate HERO information is made available to the operational commander in order that realistic balances can be established and employed between ordnance operations and the use of communication, radar, and electronic warfare transmitters.

(d) **Responsibilities**

<u>1</u>. **DON HERO Program.** As previously noted, the ship's CO has ultimate authority over embarked units in all areas involving safety of the ship or its crew. With respect to HERO safety, the Navy has well established policies and procedures to ensure safety of operations involving ordnance exposure to the EME. The DON HERO program objectives are to develop, coordinate, and direct HERO efforts to ensure that the conflict between ordnance safety and use of the EM spectrum can be effectively managed in the conduct of DON and joint-Service operations. These objectives are met primarily by the design and certification of electrically initiated ordnance to the requirements of Military Standard (MIL-STD) 464C, *Electromagnetic Environmental Effects Requirements for Systems,* and the measurement of the EME ashore and afloat as required by NAVSEA OP 3565 Volume 2, *Electromagnetic Radiation Hazards (U) (Hazards to Ordnance).* NAVSEA OP 3565 classifies ordnance types as SAFE, SUSCEPTIBLE, UNSAFE, or UNRELIABLE. It establishes separation distances between ordnance and various types of RF emitters, describes how to develop the HERO EMCON bill and provides procedures for calculating field strengths and requesting a HERO survey. Naval Sea Systems Command Instruction (NAVSEAINST) 8020.7, *Hazards of Electromagnetic Radiation to Ordnance Safety Program,* assigns NOSSA the responsibility to administer the HERO program within the DON. The NSWCDD is assigned the technical agent for the DON HERO program and provides engineering and technical support including maintaining HERO test facilities, certifying ordnance and weapon systems for use aboard ship, and providing operational HERO EMCON bills for managing ordnance operations aboard ship and at shore facilities.

<u>2</u>. **CO and Helicopter/Tiltrotor Aircraft Squadron Commander/Detachment OIC.** DOD Manual 6055.09-M, *DOD Ammunition and Explosives Safety Standards,* requires DOD components to take measures to ensure HERO issues are resolved during the planning of joint or combined operations. Measures that can minimize HERO include identifying ordnance susceptibilities, quantifying EMEs, evaluating risks associated with ordnance procedures, and establishing tailored EMCON instructions. However, when the Navy's HERO EMCON bill does not address the operational concerns on non-Navy ordnance aboard ship, the joint spectrum center ordnance electromagnetic environmental effects risk assessment database (JOERAD) should be consulted for assistance. The commanders' responsibilities include:

<u>3</u>. **Ship's CO.** The ship's CO has overall responsibility for the welfare and safety of all personnel on the ship. Although not all-inclusive, the CO's responsibilities for safe ordnance handling are:

<u>a</u>. Provide safe ordnance operations and verification of helicopter/tiltrotor aircraft detachment and personnel ordnance certifications.

<u>b</u>. Maintain a technical publications library of aviation ordnance handling, safety, and security publications, checklists, and associated Navy TYCOM instructions. These publications will normally be made available as a pre-deployment package by the TYCOM.

<u>c.</u> Stow all ammunition IAW NAVSEA OP 4, *Ammunition and Explosives Safety Afloat,* and if required, submit waivers for stowage of ammunition and obtaining approval prior to loading onboard.

<u>d.</u> Verify that all ordnance for use by the helicopter/tiltrotor aircraft unit has been approved by the WSESRB. A report is made to the TYCOM on initial receipt of all ammunition brought aboard for the aviation detachment. Monthly reports reflecting air detachment inventory will be submitted until the detachment departs. A final report will then be submitted.

<u>e.</u> Ensure that a HERO or EMCON bill is promulgated before arrival of a helicopter/tiltrotor aircraft detachment. COs will ensure that EM radiation hazards that have the potential to affect electro-explosive ordnance devices, fuel, and assigned personnel are controlled during shipboard helicopter/tiltrotor aircraft operations. The ship's HERO or EMCON bill should depict individual HERO or EMCON conditions to be set before each specific operational condition, specifically arming or de-arming, aviation ordnance movements, and fueling operations.

<u>f.</u> Establish an aviation ordnance qualification or certification board to certify the combined ship and other Service aviation ordnance team.

<u>4.</u> **Helicopter/Tiltrotor Aircraft Squadron Commander/Detachment OIC Responsibilities.** The squadron commander/detachment OIC is responsible to the ship's CO for safe aviation ordnance operations as they relate to the helicopter/tiltrotor aircraft unit. Although not all-inclusive, the squadron commander/OIC will:

<u>a.</u> Ensure that squadron/detachment personnel use Service and NAVAIR-approved aircraft system checklists and ordnance loading and downloading procedures.

<u>b.</u> Verify the qualification of assigned squadron/detachment personnel to conduct aviation ordnance operations aboard ship and present qualification or certification documentation to the ship's CO when requested.

<u>c.</u> Assist the ship's ordnance personnel in the handling and movement of aviation ordnance and related materials from the ship's magazines to designated assembly, staging or ready service, or flight deck areas as appropriate.

<u>d.</u> Provide the ship with an ammunition embarkation plan that identifies the types, quantities, number of pallets, weight, and cube of ammunition.

<u>e.</u> Provide an inventory of all personal and individual weapons.

<u>f.</u> Acquire a list of WSESRB approved weapons and explosives.

g. Upon receipt of the WSESRB list of approved weapons and explosives, certify to the ship's CO that all squadron/detachment ordnance meets WSESRB requirements for shipboard operations.

h. Ensure compliance with the ship's qualification or certification board to certify the combined ship and squadron/detachment aviation ordnance team.

(e) **HERO EMCON Bill.** A HERO EMCON bill is a set of directions for implementing HERO restrictions on ships and shore stations. Aboard ship, an EMCON bill's development and implementation are typically the responsibility of the combat system officer or the EWO. Its purpose is to prescribe operating restrictions, through advance planning, the known conflicts between the EME created by high-power transmitting equipment and HERO classified ordnance. The degree of relief from HERO EMCON restrictions that can be obtained by following a HERO EMCON bill is dependent upon two factors:

1. The amount and type of ordnance that is involved, and

2. Knowledge of the ambient RF environment at locations where exposure occurs during presence, handling, loading, storage, assembly, and transportation operations.

(f) Once the EMCON bill is established, appropriate separation distances must be maintained between fixed emitter systems and inbound and outbound aircraft carrying HERO SUSCEPTIBLE and HERO UNSAFE/UNRELIABLE ordnance. This process may also result in the silencing of communications and high-power search and fire control radars.

(g) The ship requires information concerning the exact ordnance the embarking unit will be loading aboard. This information is important both for the ship's ordnance personnel to plan where and how to store it, but also for ship operators to determine other safety factors. As noted in the listing of responsibilities of the squadron commander/detachment OIC, the embarking squadron/detachment must declare all ordnance and emitter items to the ship's CO. This information will allow any required changes to be made to the ship's EMCON bill due to the introduction of the embarking squadron's/detachment's ordnance loadout. The embarking unit provides a detailed list of all ordnance to be deployed aboard the ship with the following information as soon as the mission has been identified. Items on the list include:

1. DODIC or NALC: Ammunition is identified by a DODIC or a NALC.

2. Quantities: Total amount for each DODIC.

3. Stock Numbers: NSN, which will be used for locating more information on each item.

<u>4.</u> Lot Numbers: ALN or SN.

<u>5.</u> Hazard Classification: Department of Transportation code issued to all ordnance items used to determine storage segregation for HAZMAT.

<u>6.</u> Container Dimensions: The dimensions of ammunition containers as separate items and also as a palletized load both to ensure adequate storage space and to determine how the ship will load as combat cargo.

<u>7.</u> Additionally, a list of all small arms the unit is bringing.

(h) NAVSEA OP 3565 Volume 2, *Electromagnetic Radiation Hazards (U) (Hazards to Ordnance),* addresses HERO EMCON requirements and procedures in detail. A HERO survey is usually required to develop the HERO EMCON bill. This survey provides measured data on the shipboard EME along with detailed information on the configuration, status, and operational procedures of RF transmitters and ordnance items.

(3) **HERF and HERP**

(a) **HERF.** HERF is the potential hazard that is created when volatile combustibles, such as fuel, are exposed to EM fields of sufficient energy to cause ignition. To reduce the possibility of fuel vapor ignition by high-powered transmitters or other spark sources, the Navy uses jet propulsion fuel, type 5 (JP5) exclusively aboard ship. Typically, most Army and Air Force units use jet propulsion fuel, type 8 (JP8), or jet propulsion fuel, type 4 (JP4), which have a lower flash point than JP5 and are therefore considered more susceptible to shipboard E3. Aircraft containing JP8 fuel may operate aboard Navy ships, to include launch/recovery, startup/shutdown, and refueling. Aircraft with fuels other than JP5 are requested to notify the ship's air officer "air boss" prior to landing, so appropriate precautions may be taken by flight deck personnel. Aircraft containing fuel other than JP5 will not be allowed in the ship's hangar. If shipboard hangaring of nonorganic aircraft is anticipated, embarking helicopters/tiltrotor aircraft should make every effort to fill all aircraft tanks with JP5 fuel prior to arrival on the ship (available at most Navy airfields). If this is not possible, the aircraft will be refueled on the flight deck with JP5, and fuel samples will be drawn and flash point tested. The aircraft will not be hangared until all samples test at 120°Fahrenheit (F) or higher. In the absence of flash point testing, aircraft arriving with fuel other than JP5 will not be permitted in the hangar until they have been refueled at least three times with JP5. For more specific information, consult NAVAIR 00-80T-109, *Aircraft Refueling NATOPS Manual.*

(b) **HERP.** HERP is the potential hazard that exists when personnel are exposed to an EM field of sufficient intensity to heat the human body. If the body's heat gain exceeds its ability to rid itself of excess heat, an increase in body temperature can occur that could have an effect on metabolic processes, with potentially deleterious effects. Radiation from high-powered transmitters can cause injury to personnel in the vicinity of transmitting antennas located on the ship's deck and masts. Stand-off areas around high-powered RF antennas are clearly marked on the ship's decks and bulkheads with a bright red circle. Since it is not possible to visibly determine if an antenna is transmitting, personnel should avoid entering these stand-off areas at all times. Exposure to excessive levels of RF radiation may not produce a noticeable feeling of pain or heat to warn that injury is occurring. Avoid entry into marked stand-off areas.

(4) **EMCON and EMV**

(a) This section covers the EMCON and EMV information that is necessary to prepare for compatible and interference-free shipboard helicopter/tiltrotor operations. Some non-maritime helicopters/tiltrotor aircraft have not been tested in the EME of various ship classes. When conducting non-USN operations, consideration must be given to potential radiation hazards, EMI, and EMV.

(b) Joint operations increase the potential for undesired E3, particularly if the platforms and their associated systems and equipment are exposed to operational EMEs different from those for which they were designed and tested. When helicopters/tiltrotor aircraft are operating in the vicinity of ships, there must be established guidelines and procedures to avoid or minimize the potential for harmful EMI to shipboard, avionics, engine, and flight control systems. This guidance provides platform distance separation restrictions, along with radar main-beam illumination restrictions to preclude "burnout" and/or performance degradation of sensitive electronic components aboard the aircraft. The preparation and implementation of an effective HERO EMCON bill will also assist in the control of EMI during operational deployments.

(c) In an effort to mitigate E3 on joint service helicopters/tiltrotor aircraft, numerous EMV tests have been conducted on Army and Air Force airframes. Many Army helicopters can obtain shipboard transmitter guidance from the aircraft's high intensity radio transmission area (HIRTA) messages. The negative effects of shipboard transmitters is known and documented in EMV reports, but these are not published in an operator-friendly format; however, this information is contained in JOERAD, to provide complete E3 information for the embarked unit and the ship's company.

# CHAPTER III
## OPERATIONS

*"If you are in trouble anywhere in the world, an airplane can fly over and drop flowers, but a helicopter can land and save your life."*

**Igor Sikorsky, 1947**

## 1. Pre-Operations

a. Helicopter/tiltrotor aircraft operations from ships place both ship and flight personnel in a unique and demanding environment. Close coordination and proper actions are required by all personnel at all times. Operational effectiveness and flight safety require extensive training in the areas of C2, aircraft coordination, and flight deck procedures. In order to provide the required amount of teamwork and enhance flight safety, the air officer, aviation officer, squadron commander, detachment OIC, or a designated officer shall conduct the following briefings:

(1) **Commanding Officer and Executive Officer.** The CO and XO will receive a thorough brief from the air or aviation department head and the commander/OIC of the Service helicopter/tiltrotor aircraft squadron/detachment. This briefing will cover, but should not be limited to, aircraft capabilities, planned training, and operational evolutions, with impact on ship's schedule and waiver requirements emphasized. Particular emphasis will be placed on the relation of each evolution to normal operations and any waiver requirements.

(2) **Helicopter Control Officer.** An HCO is a designated helicopter pilot or a graduate of the helicopter indoctrination course. In nonaviation facility ships, the HCO will be responsible for the supervision and direction of launching and landing operations and for servicing and handling of all embarked helicopters/tiltrotor aircraft. The HCO or air officer will thoroughly brief the commander/OIC of the helicopter/tiltrotor aircraft unit before commencing joint flight operations. This brief will cover, but is not limited to the following:

(a) Radio communications and terminology. See recommended brevity codes in FM 1-02.1/MCRP 3-25G/NTTP 6-02.1/AFTTP(I) 3-2.5, *Multi-Service Brevity Codes.*

(b) Light and hand signals.

(c) Aircraft configuration, including fueling, armament, TD, and rescue specifics.

(d) NVD procedures and operating techniques.

(e) Emergency procedures.

(3) **Ship's Air or Aviation Officer, Flight Deck Officer or Director, and Flight Deck Cargo Supervisor.** Key air operations personnel will be briefed on planned operations by the ship's operations officer. Coordination of flight deck evolutions and operation-specific procedures will be covered in detail.

(4) **Officer of the Deck (OOD).** All OODs will be briefed by the air or aviation department head and operations officer regarding specific limitations on deck movement, wind envelopes, and the ship's light configuration.

(5) **Engineer Officer or Aviation Fuels Officer.** These officers will be briefed by the embarked unit with regard to the type of fuel to be brought aboard by the Service units, fuel requirements, and fueling or defueling procedures once aboard. Particular attention will be paid to the hazards of JP8 and its effect on storage risks, volatility of mixtures, and fire fighting considerations. The engineering or aviation fuels officer is responsible for routine fuel sample inspections and will provide a fuel sample for the helicopter/tiltrotor aircraft commander during "hot refuelings" (refueling with engines, auxiliary power units, and/or rotors in operation).

(6) **Crash Crew or Fire Party On-Scene Leader.** Fire fighting and rescue personnel will be briefed by the embarked detachment regarding aircraft particulars as they pertain to rescue and salvage operations. Once embarked for operations, the helicopter/tiltrotor aircraft units will provide the weapons officer and crash crew personnel with orientation lectures on rescue access, armament safing, ordnance, fire fighting hazards, and aircraft emergency shutdown procedures.

(7) **LSO or LSE.** The LSO or LSE will be briefed by the embarked unit on special requirements with regard to lighting, signals, NVDs, aircraft securing, and fueling operations.

(8) **Air Controllers and Combat Information Center Personnel.** Air control personnel will be briefed by the operations officer with regard to communications and identification equipment, SAR capabilities, weather criteria, and instrument approach procedures.

(9) **Weapons Department Personnel.** Weapons department personnel will be briefed by the embarked unit on the characteristics of all aviation ordnance planned for employment, loading/arming/safing procedures and inherent design safety features of the ordnance and aircraft systems of each aircraft planned for embarkation. Non-Navy embarking units will provide training to ship's weapons personnel on ordnance when requested by the ship following the presail conference.

(10) **Flight Deck Personnel.** Flight deck personnel, including the ordnance officer, or the designated ordnance subject matter expert will be briefed by the embarked unit on platform-specific procedures for fueling and deck handling evolutions, including procedures for the use of NVDs if their use is planned.

(11) **Ship's Company Briefs.** When applicable, the ship's company will be briefed by the executive department regarding operations security aspects and restrictive lighting measures, including the lighting hazards during NVD operations.

b. **Command and Control Spaces.** Most Navy ships are not configured with C2 spaces for embarked Army or Air Force units. The embarked unit command element will be required to share already-cramped shipboard C2 spaces. Units such as SOF that desire a special compartment information facility for planning should make this requirement known early in the pre-deployment planning process as these facilities are limited in number and size, particularly on ACS.

c. **Communications Equipment.** Some embarked units will bring their own portable communications equipment. While having their own communications pathways can ease competition for scarce shipboard resources, antenna location must be coordinated. Additionally, possible interference with shipboard electronics and EMCON policies must be considered and carefully coordinated.

## 2. Shipboard Command Authorities

a. **Ship's Commanding Officer.** USN and USCG regulations set forth the authority of the ship's CO with respect to aircraft embarked in or operating from the ship. When operating with a helicopter/tiltrotor aircraft unit embarked, the joint force commander's (JFC's) operation order will define command relationships for the assigned mission. These command relationships will normally apply from initial embarkation until final debarkation. In all cases, the ship's CO retains authority over embarked units in all areas involving safety of the ship or its crew.

b. **Embarked Unit's Commander/Officer in Charge.** An embarked unit commander/detachment OIC shall be designated by the JFC or the parent unit's commanding officer. The designated commander/OIC reports directly to the ship's CO, air wing commander, or authority specified by the JFC for the mission assigned. Administratively, the commander/OIC normally reports to the ship's XO for matters of day-to-day routine with respect to the embarked unit while embarked on the ship. When embarked on an air-capable or amphibious aviation assault ship, the commander/OIC reports to the officer specified in the appropriate tasking order regarding the assigned mission and administrative routine. Normal procedure will be for the organic helicopter squadron on the aircraft carrier to act as host and provide liaison between the ship and the embarked unit. The commander/OIC has the authority and responsibility for the following:

(1) Initiate coordination for a presail conference. (See sample checklist in Appendix C, "Pre-Deployment Planning Checklists.")

(2) Coordinate embarked unit embarkation requirements with the XO of the ship.

(3) Provide certification documents to the ship's CO on the embarked unit's completion of presail.

(4) Coordinate all requirements for communications to higher authority with the ship's CO.

(5) Apprise the ship's CO and operations officer of operational and support requirements that directly affect the ship's operations.

(6) Apprise the ship's CO of embarked unit's readiness when required for operational reporting requirements to higher authority.

(7) Ensure embarked unit compliance with ship's routine operating and administrative instructions.

## 3. Flight and Hangar Deck Operations

The ship's CO has overall responsibility for all actions that take place on a ship to include the flight and hangar decks. Limited space and the potential for conducting numerous varied and hazardous tasks simultaneously require close control and coordination to ensure that operations are conducted safely. Flight and hangar decks are hazardous work areas. Constant vigilance is required to prevent personal injury or helicopter/tiltrotor aircraft or other equipment damage during flight and hangar deck operations. The embarked unit should plan on providing a noncommissioned officer as flight deck liaison to facilitate close coordination with the ship's personnel.

a. Immediately after embarkation, the unit should expect to attend a general shipboard safety brief. This brief should also include the conduct expected of personnel while on the flight and hangar decks. Aircrews and maintenance personnel can expect a more specific flight and hangar deck orientation brief prior to beginning their operations in these areas. The risks associated with conducting daily flight and hangar deck operations aboard ship can be minimized through effective communication and coordination between ship's personnel and embarked personnel.

b. The combination of relative winds and rotor downwash when launching or landing a helicopter/tiltrotor aircraft immediately adjacent to a spot occupied by a shutdown helicopter/tiltrotor aircraft may cause rotor system damage to the shutdown helicopter/tiltrotor aircraft. Blade fold systems of helicopters designed for land operations are designed for aircraft transport or storage only. Extreme care shall be taken when launching or recovering helicopters/tiltrotor aircraft immediately adjacent to a spot occupied by these helicopters. Rotor downwash created by the CH-47, CH-53E, and the V-22 is greater than that produced by any other embarked helicopter. This downwash is sufficient to damage unsecured rotor blades and to blow aircraft chocks, tiedown chains, and towbars about the deck or overboard, and cause personnel injury or death. Because of the susceptibility of the AH/MH-6 helicopter to wind-related damage, launches and recoveries to a spot immediately upwind or crosswind from a static AH/MH-6 (blades unsecured, tied down, or folded) should not be conducted except in case of an emergency.

c. **Post Landing, Shutdown, and Blade Fold**

(1) **Post Landing.** All post landing events will be controlled by/coordinated with appropriate ship's personnel. After landing, expect the following sequence of events in preparation for shutdown:

(a) The helicopter/tiltrotor aircraft will be chocked and chained.

(b) Cargo and personnel will be unloaded.

(c) The helicopter/tiltrotor aircraft will be shut down, unless it will be launching again.

(d) The helicopter/tiltrotor aircraft will be refueled (time and fuel state permitting).

(e) Any required immediate action maintenance will be performed (time permitting).

(2) **Shutdown.** Engine shutdown and rotor disengagement aboard ship can be more difficult and more hazardous than ashore, especially for helicopters that do not have a rotor brake. High winds and a rolling/pitching flight deck, coupled with the geometric design of ships and their superstructures, can cause unusual wind patterns (accelerated updrafts and downdrafts) in the helicopter shutdown area. Helicopters not equipped with a rotor brake may experience rotor coast-down times in excess of five minutes, as well as rotor blade flex and flap as the rotor RPM slows. It is not unusual for the main rotor blades to flap downward to within two feet of the flight deck or to flap up in excess of 45 degrees during a no rotor brake shut down. This excess flapping can cause damage to rotor head components and is a potential safety hazard to personnel. Prior to no-rotor brake shutdowns, the ship should strive to obtain the minimum winds across the deck and should also keep other helicopters from landing on or departing from adjacent spots in order to reduce the possibility of helicopter component damage and/or personnel injury.

(3) **Blade Fold.** Folding or spreading main rotor blades may be required to conserve flight deck space, use the ship's elevator, or to hangar the aircraft. Tiltrotor aircraft are equipped with an automatic blade fold and wing stow system. Typically, automatic blade fold systems are designed to fold helicopter main rotor blades in less than two minutes. Army helicopters do not have automatic blade fold systems. However, most Army helicopters have the capability to fold their blades manually. Manual blade fold times vary depending on the type of helicopter and the proficiency of the fold crew. In general, the smaller the helicopter the quicker and easier it is to fold. The MH-6 can fold rotor blades in less than 10 minutes while the MH-47 typically takes 40 minutes or longer to fold rotor blades. Manual blade fold procedures may require repositioning of the helicopter on the flight deck to ensure that blade walkers will be able to remain safely on the flight deck while walking blades to the folded position. Close coordination and understanding between the ship's personnel and helicopter unit is required to determine blade fold capabilities and develop launch/recovery timelines. The effects of wind speed and direction, combined with ship motion, can adversely affect the ability to control the blades. Crews must exercise

extreme caution when folding or spreading blades in high wind/deck motion conditions. It is highly recommended that maintenance crews practice manual blade fold/spread procedures prior to embarkation. It is also recommended that the specific helicopter that will be embarked on the ship conduct at least one blade fold/spread evolution prior to embarkation to ensure that rotor head pins, nuts, bolts, etc., are serviceable and move freely and easily.

> **Note: Army/Air Force blade fold support systems are not designed for the high winds and turbulence routinely encountered on the flight deck of a ship underway. Personnel should reference aircraft operations manuals to ensure blade fold support systems rotor blades, and/or rotor heads are not damaged by winds or when in close proximity to launching/recovering aircraft. The V-22 maximum safe relative wind conditions for folding or unfolding the proprotor blades and wing stow/unstow is 45 knots from any quadrant.**
>
> **Note: Electromagnetic interference from SPS-40 and SPS-49 radars may cause the blade fold planetary tube shear pins to break during blade fold and wing stow.**

d. **Shipboard Refuel/Defuel.** JP5 is required by the Navy for shipboard operations because of its higher flash point compared to other types of jet fuel. If possible, aircrew should plan to arrive aboard ship with only JP5 in their fuel tanks.

e. **Shipboard Helicopter/Tiltrotor Aircraft Deck Handling/Movement.** Safe, efficient helicopter/tiltrotor aircraft movement aboard ship is a joint effort between ship's personnel and the helicopter/tiltrotor aircraft unit's personnel. After coordination has been accomplished, the ship will provide a qualified move director and move crew. The helicopter/tiltrotor aircraft unit will provide a plane captain or crew chief to act as a brake rider and/or unit safety observer. The embarked unit should provide ship's personnel with a helicopter/tiltrotor aircraft orientation brief prior to handling/movement operations because ship's personnel may not be familiar with other Service helicopters/tiltrotor aircraft. At a minimum, the orientation brief should cover TD points, grounding points, movement procedures, refuel/defuel procedures, unique features, and aircrew emergency access/rescue procedures. Care should be taken when spotting or stacking V-22s to avoid damage from engine exhaust to antennas and radomes. Deck heating from aircraft nacelles should be minimized whenever possible by reducing the inboard engine to idle and especially if on-deck delay is expected to be greater than 15 minutes. The inboard engine should be shut down if delay time is to exceed 30 minutes.

f. On ACSs without air departments, helicopter/tiltrotor aircraft movement and handling will be conducted manually (personnel will push the helicopter/tiltrotor aircraft to the desired location). On ships with air departments (aircraft carriers, AASs, and amphibious transport docks), helicopter/tiltrotor aircraft movement/handling is usually performed with tow bars, tow tractors, or other Navy GSE provided by the ship. Any special equipment requirements for helicopter/tiltrotor aircraft movement must be arranged with the ship. The embarking unit should be prepared to provide required specialized handling equipment. Severe weather, high winds (normally in excess of 45 knots relative) and/or high sea state may preclude all helicopter/tiltrotor aircraft movement/handling.

g. **Pre-Takeoff Procedures.** Based upon the air plan and flight schedule, the ship will man its flight quarters stations in time to meet the first scheduled launch. The ship and the helicopter/tiltrotor aircraft unit will be conducting independent and coordinated actions in preparation for helicopter/tiltrotor aircraft launch. Each ship and embarked unit should establish the pre-takeoff sequence that best supports their operations and the assigned mission. A notional sequence of events in support of the initial launch of helicopter/tiltrotor aircraft is listed below; these recommended times may be reduced as ship and unit personnel gain experience working together:

(1) Pilot/aircrew brief (approximately 120 minutes prior to launch time).

(2) Ship personnel man flight quarter stations (approximately 30 to 90 minutes prior to launch time). All ATC, fueling, fire fighting, and helicopter/tiltrotor aircraft movement/handling stations are manned. This time may need to be adjusted depending on the requirement to manually spread rotors and/or conduct ordnance evolutions.

(3) Ship calls for FOD walk-down (approximately 60 minutes prior to launch time).

(4) Pilots/aircrews conduct preflight inspections (approximately 45 minutes prior to launch time).

(5) Pilots/aircrew man helicopter/tiltrotor aircraft (30 minutes prior to launch time pilots in their seats).

(6) Ship obtains necessary winds for start. Helicopter/tiltrotor aircraft engines started and rotors engaged (15 minutes prior to launch time). Radio checks complete.

(7) Ship obtains winds for launch. Helicopter/tiltrotor aircraft loaded (10 minutes prior to launch time).

(8) All helicopters/tiltrotor aircraft: chocks and chains removed (1 to 3 minutes prior to launch time).

(9) Helicopter/tiltrotor aircraft launched on time IAW the air plan/flight schedule.

h. **Spread Rotors/Proprotors and Start-Up**

(1) **Spreading Rotors.** Most helicopters/tiltrotor aircraft have the capability to fold and spread rotor blades or proprotors. The spread procedures are much the same as the fold procedures, but they are conducted in reverse order. Embarked units will need to coordinate and schedule the rotor spread evolution to ensure completion in time to support

the air plan and flight schedule. Manual blade spread will require the helicopter to be positioned so each blade can be walked into position by maintenance personnel. Once again, in general terms, the smaller helicopter will be able to spread its blades more rapidly than the larger helicopter.

(2) **Helicopter/Tiltrotor Aircraft Start-Up and Rotor Engagement.** Helicopter/tiltrotor aircraft engines/auxiliary power units shall not be started without the ship's permission. It is the ship's personnel responsibility, through coordination with the embarked unit, to ensure that aircrews have the winds required for a safe engine start and rotor engagement for their specific helicopter/tiltrotor aircraft. During initial engine start and rotor engagement, the low inertia/speed of the main helicopter rotor blades will permit rotor blades to flex and flap as they rotate. As the velocity of the relative wind increases, the likelihood of the blades flexing and flapping will also increase. Caution should be observed during this stage of rotor engagement to keep personnel outside and well clear of the rotor arc. Prior to rotor start-ups, the ship should strive to obtain minimum winds across the deck and should also preclude other helicopters from landing on and/or departing from adjacent spots in order to reduce the possibility of helicopter component damage and/or personnel injury. H-1 and V-22 aircraft engage rotors simultaneously with engine start. V-22 aircraft may engage or disengage rotors with the ship in a turn and wind conditions within the engage/disengage wind envelope established in the applicable NATOPS.

(3) The aircrew must inform the ship once the pre-takeoff checks are complete and the helicopter/tiltrotor aircraft is ready for takeoff. Following this notification, the ship will provide the relative winds for takeoff and will remove the chocks and chains from the helicopter/tiltrotor aircraft. The helicopter/tiltrotor aircraft is now ready for takeoff, pending clearance from the air boss, under the direction of the LSE. On LHA/LHD class ships, launch/recovery of V-22s shall be conducted from/to H-53 mainmount wheel boxes.

i. **General Fueling Procedures.** Helicopter/tiltrotor aircraft fueling operations on ships are classified as either cold refueling (engines off) or hot refueling (rotors/proprotors turning or engines operating). Cold refueling may be accomplished by pressure or gravity. Hot refueling is limited to pressure fueling only. Shipboard fueling and defueling procedures may be found in NAVAIR 00-80T-109, *Aircraft Refueling NATOPS Manual,* and NAVAIR 00-80T-122, *Helicopter Operating Procedures for Air-Capable Ships NATOPS Manual.*

(1) **Fuel Compatibility.** To reduce the hazard of shipboard fires, only fuel with a flash point above 140°F is permitted to be stored aboard ships. USA and USAF aircraft use JP8 (or their NATO/civilian equivalents which may include JP4) as their first choice for fuel, although all can operate with JP5. Since Army and Air Force shore installations typically do not provide JP5 fuel—and Navy aviation refueling installations are not always available—it may not always be possible for helicopters/tiltrotor aircraft to transition to JP5 prior to arriving at the ship. In addition, Navy safety doctrine prohibits the hangaring of helicopters/tiltrotor aircraft with significant quantities of JP4 or JP8 in their tanks because of the low flash points of those fuels. Furthermore, JP4 and JP8 cannot be introduced into ship JP5 fuel tanks because of concerns about lowering the flash point of the fuel stock and

introduction of additives (such as "Plus 100") that adversely affect the ability of Navy shipboard filtration systems to remove water from the fuel. Because JP5 is not universally available on shore, helicopters/tiltrotor aircraft are likely to arrive at the ship with significant quantities of JP4 or JP8 in their systems, especially in short notice operations. This presents a problem if it is necessary to immediately hangar the helicopter/tiltrotor aircraft (high winds, maintenance). In this case, the choice is to defuel the aircraft or introduce enough JP5 into the helicopter's/tiltrotor aircraft fuel tanks to raise the flash point to acceptable limits; defueling may be required to allow for the addition of JP5. Unless the ship is equipped with a holding tank to contain the discarded fuel, the only alternative will be to defuel the aircraft to the environment, which may not be a viable option, depending upon local environmental protection regulations. Therefore, if a ship is expected to operate with helicopters/tiltrotor aircraft designed for land operations, it should be equipped with the capability to defuel JP4 or JP8 to a holding tank, or otherwise dispose of it. For exceptional circumstances, procedures for hangaring helicopters/tiltrotor aircraft with other than JP5 may be found in NAVAIR-00-80T-106, *LHA/LHD NATOPS Manual*. The following procedures should be used to raise the flash point to the desired level:

(a) **Preferred Procedure.** Defuel helicopter/tiltrotor aircraft completely and refuel with JP5. Ships have limited ability to handle hazardous waste; therefore, this procedure should be done ashore prior to embarking on the ship.

(b) **Alternate Method.** Helicopter/tiltrotor aircraft should burn down to minimum fuel and refuel with JP5 after landing (an alternate method for AAS and CVN is to use the plane-to-plane transfer cart available on AAS and CVN).

(c) Neither procedure is guaranteed to raise the flash point. The ship will take fuel samples and determine flash point prior to hangaring the helicopter/tiltrotor aircraft. It may be necessary to repeat the procedures several times.

(2) **Refueling Equipment.** Not all helicopters are equipped with single point pressure refueling systems as in the Navy. Some of them rely upon CCR (gravity fueling with nozzle/tank fitting adapter to capture fumes) and/or open-port fueling to fill some or all of their fuel tanks. In addition, some of their aircraft cannot CCR fuel at pressures greater than 15 psi, whereas current Navy capability is to CCR at a minimum of 45 psi.

(3) **Hot Refueling Aircraft with Ordnance.** Aircraft with ordnance are not normally hot refueled onboard ships. When all required HERO precautions have been met, the ship's CO may authorize ordnance-equipped helicopters to be hot refueled when required by operational necessity.

Intentionally Blank

# CHAPTER IV
## SUSTAINMENT

## 1. General

a. **Deck Handling/Maneuvering/Spotting.** Space is very limited aboard ship, with aircraft required to share takeoff, landing, and maintenance spots. Therefore, helicopters/tiltrotor aircraft may need to be repositioned frequently and expeditiously, often on a windy, wet, and moving deck in close proximity to other aircraft and ship's structure. When not being repositioned, aircraft must be chained to the flight deck in order to prevent unintended movement due to wind and ship motion. Helicopter/tiltrotor aircraft space requirements and ease of handling largely determine the number of aircraft that a ship can accommodate and, in turn, have a major impact upon the tempo and effectiveness of operations.

b. Helicopters designed for land operations typically require more space than helicopters designed for maritime operations. Most do not have automatic blade folding systems but do have limited manual blade fold capability to enable transportation aboard ship or aircraft. These manual fold systems are typically not designed for quick and easy folds, nor are they robust enough to withstand high winds. Damage to folded rotor systems can occur in less than 25 knots of relative wind. The landing gear geometry and towing systems of helicopters designed for land operations are not optimized for maneuvering in tight spaces. The aircraft TD points may not be designed to deal with the stresses associated with high winds and deck movement. Therefore, these helicopters may require special handling when maneuvering, spotting, and parking.

c. Personnel are trained to maneuver embarked maritime helicopters/tiltrotor aircraft using the support equipment embarked. It may be necessary to alter established practices when using shipboard support equipment with helicopter/tiltrotor aircraft designed for land operations because of their limitations and compatibility with shipboard configurations. Embarked unit maintenance personnel should brief shipboard handlers on the appropriate procedures and established practices for handling their particular T/M/S of helicopter/tiltrotor aircraft. Among the issues that should be addressed are:

(1) Towing systems: Which tow tractors and tow bars are compatible with, or acceptable for use with the embarking helicopter/tiltrotor aircraft?

(2) Aircraft mooring/chaining system (aircraft physical security): location of the helicopter/tiltrotor aircraft TD points and how the helicopter/tiltrotor aircraft is to be secured.

(3) Blades folded mooring system limitations: USA and USAF blade TD systems are designed to hold the blades for an air transport, not for heavy weather security.

(4) Blade or tail fold provisions and requirements.

(5) Blade removal requirements.

(6) Special handling equipment.

*Information on the above can be obtained from specific aircraft maintenance manuals, but is more easily obtained by discussion with the unit at the presail conference.*

## 2. Maintenance Considerations

Conducting aircraft maintenance aboard ship requires detailed planning and coordination. Issues to consider include ship movement and environmental conditions; space, time, weather, and lighting constraints; safety requirements; availability of repairable items and consumable parts and supplies; calibration requirements; and the inherent maintenance capability of the ship.

a. **General.** Most shipboard helicopter/tiltrotor aircraft maintenance must be conducted on the flight deck of the ship. Flight decks are exposed to the elements and are in constant motion due to changing sea states. As a result, helicopter/tiltrotor aircraft maintenance can be extremely hazardous at all times, but especially at night, in inclement weather, or when flight operations are in progress. On multispot ships, helicopter/tiltrotor aircraft maintenance can be extremely difficult and/or hazardous during flight operations. Each class/type ship has different helicopter/tiltrotor aircraft maintenance support capabilities and procedures.

b. **Maintenance Facilities.** Available aviation maintenance facilities vary widely with ship class. NAEC-ENG-7576, *Shipboard Aviation Facilities Resume,* provides guidance regarding ACSs. Aircraft carriers and AASs have extensive maintenance facilities, including an aircraft intermediate maintenance department (AIMD), which is capable of a wide range of functions. These functions include, but are not limited to, electronics repair, tire and wheel buildup, composite material repair, oxygen servicing, and inspection and repair of aircrew survival equipment. However, support for particular systems is not assured and should be determined in advance. JFCs are responsible for coordinating required maintenance infrastructure.

c. **Aircraft Carrier Maintenance Capabilities.** Although a great deal of helicopter/tiltrotor aircraft maintenance may be performed on the flight deck of an aircraft carrier, the large deck edge elevators, large hangar door openings, and large hangars make it relatively easy to move most helicopters/tiltrotor aircraft to/from the hangar deck for maintenance. All Army and Air Force helicopters may be moved from the flight deck to the hangar deck with blades spread (it should be noted that this is not the preferred method for ship's personnel). Presail planning and/or coordination with the ship should determine specific helicopter/tiltrotor aircraft certifications for elevator and hangar deck operations. The hangar deck is well lighted, protected from the elements, contains overhead hoists, and has support equipment available.

(1) Aircraft carriers have a robust AIMD that is capable of providing third- and fourth-echelon maintenance. The AIMD is capable of providing repairs for airframe structures, hydraulic systems, fuel cells, avionics/weapons systems, and corrosion control, as well as engine buildup and testing.

(2) Although the AIMD is designed to support Navy aircraft, their expertise may be of great benefit to an embarked unit, especially in terms of corrosion control, airframes, hydraulics, and special tool fabrication. Additionally, aircraft carriers have spaces designed as maintenance workspaces. In the event that a helicopter/tiltrotor aircraft unit will be embarked for an extended period of time, the embarked unit may want to augment the ship's AIMD with personnel expertise and/or test/calibration equipment.

d. **AAS Maintenance Capabilities.** Large amphibious ships have the same type of maintenance capabilities as the aircraft carrier, although in a somewhat smaller package. AASs have a smaller flight deck, smaller elevators, smaller hangar door openings, and smaller hangars than aircraft carriers. Much like the aircraft carrier, the hangar deck of the AAS is well lighted, protected from the elements, contains overhead hoists, and has support equipment available. All heavy helicopter/tiltrotor maintenance should be conducted on the hangar deck if possible. AASs also have a robust AIMD with similar capabilities and expertise as aircraft carriers.

e. **ACS Maintenance Capabilities.** An embarking unit will find limited helicopter/tiltrotor aircraft maintenance support available on these types of ships. Normally, the smaller classes of ships do not have maintenance spaces available and most maintenance is performed on the exposed flight deck. Hangars, if available, have been designed for specific organic helicopters and are extremely limited in size and capability. There is no AIMD onboard these ships. Additionally, landing ship dock class ships should be augmented with a cadre of experienced, aviation rated naval personnel prior to conducting sustained shipboard helicopter/tiltrotor operations.

f. **Maintenance Procedures.** Normal land-based helicopter/tiltrotor aircraft maintenance procedures must be examined and, where required, modified for shipboard operations. As an example, extreme caution should be used when jacking a helicopter/tiltrotor aircraft aboard ship. Even in calm seas a rapid turn by the ship could dislodge a jack and cause the helicopter/tiltrotor aircraft to fall. Additionally, work around procedures for helicopters/tiltrotor aircraft that possess avionics equipment that cannot be tested/calibrated on a moving platform will need to be addressed. Finally, as previously mentioned, most helicopter/tiltrotor aircraft maintenance will be conducted on the exposed flight deck. Procedures for working on a wet helicopter/tiltrotor aircraft in high winds and rough seas will need to be addressed. It is important to remember that all flight and hangar deck maintenance evolutions (movement, using deck edge power, using GSE, starting an auxiliary power unit, etc.) must be coordinated with and approved by the ship. The ship and the embarked unit should identify the personnel responsible for conducting maintenance coordination as soon as possible after embarkation. General POCs are listed in Figures II-1, II-2, and II-3.

g. **Post Maintenance Check Flight (PMCF).** PMCFs must be either scheduled on the daily air plan and unit flight schedule or coordinated between the embarked unit and the ship on an emergent basis. PMCFs are normally accomplished prior to the first launch, after the last launch, or between normal launch and recovery cycles. Due to the requirement to adhere to the air plan/flight schedule, aircrews conducting PMCF should be prepared to meet their requirements in the minimum time necessary while maintaining safe flight operations.

h. **Corrosion Prevention and Control.** The shipboard environment is inherently corrosive. Embarked aircraft will require cleaning and treatment for corrosion more frequently than shore-based aircraft. When at sea, embarked units must place special emphasis on the importance of a dynamic corrosion prevention and control program and ensure that it receives priority for timely accomplishment along with other required maintenance. The frequency and content of a program for inspecting, cleaning, corrosion control, and preservation of aircraft and support equipment should be established prior to commencing embarked operations.

i. **Support Equipment.** Each ACS will have an allotted individual material requirements list (IMRL) that lists the special tools, test equipment, and GSE available on that specific ship. Additionally, each ACS will have an aviation consolidated allowance list (AVCAL) that lists the aviation supply items carried on that specific ship. The IMRL and AVCAL are excellent resources to compare the ship's special tools, equipment, and supplies to the embarking unit's requirements to reduce the overall footprint of the embarking unit.

j. **Aircraft Security.** The weather at sea can be more severe than that normally encountered ashore. Ships frequently have relative winds greater than 45 knots across the flight deck. High winds can cause damage to rotor blades, rotor heads, and rotor head components, especially if the rotor blades are not properly secured/tied down. Severe pitch and roll can cause inadequately secured helicopters/tiltrotor aircraft to slide on the deck and to hit other helicopters/tiltrotor aircraft or the ship's structures.

(1) The responsibility for the helicopter/tiltrotor aircraft physical security rests with the embarked unit. Embarking units should coordinate with the ship to ensure sufficient Navy TD-1 TD chains are available to secure the unit's aircraft. Army MB-1 mooring hardware is not compatible for shipboard use. Due to the harsh at-sea environment, constant monitoring of the security of the helicopter's rotor blades/tiltrotor aircraft proprotor and the security of helicopter/tiltrotor aircraft TD chains is required. To reduce the potential for a shipboard fire, all helicopters/tiltrotor aircraft should be constantly monitored for fuel and other fluid leaks while aboard ship.

(2) The ship should require the embarked unit to provide an "aircraft integrity watch" when the ship is not at flight quarters to monitor helicopter/tiltrotor aircraft security.

It is important that personnel assigned to this watch are thoroughly instructed by the ship on the procedures and responsibilities associated with their position. The aircraft integrity watch is responsible for the security of all aircraft and equipment on the flight deck and hangar bays. The individual watch stander should routinely check each aircraft to ensure that it is not leaking petroleum, oils, and lubricants (POL) on the deck and is properly secured (airframe chained to the deck and rotor blades tied down).

k. **Safety.** The ship's safety orientation and flight deck safety briefs and the embarked unit helicopter/tiltrotor aircraft familiarization brief should be given prior to the start of flight operations.

(1) Helicopter/tiltrotor aircraft maintenance onboard ship can be very hazardous. Performing maintenance on a rotor head, on the flight deck, at night, in a 25-knot wind, in the rain, on a pitching and rolling ship is extremely hazardous. Proper flight deck safety equipment, the buddy system, adequate supervision, and safety observers will aid in reducing risks. Procedures for shipboard maintenance should be addressed and established in advance.

(2) Maintenance personnel should be provided and should wear proper flight deck safety equipment. While working on the flight deck, maintenance personnel should wear flotation equipment, head protection, hearing protection, and eye protection. The embarking unit should not rely on the ship to provide this equipment but should bring it with them.

## 3. Other Logistics and Personnel Service Considerations

a. **Background.** The purpose of this section is to outline general procedures for providing material support for helicopter/tiltrotor aircraft units assigned to joint operations. The scope and details of the implementation of these procedures are highly dependent on the duration and circumstances of a particular exercise or mission. A short-duration detachment will usually draw the bulk of its supply material from a packup kit provided by the parent Service. Resupply of drawn material will occur as needed. Material support for detachments of longer duration will be better served by establishing an independent unit identity, especially when shipboard operations will be conducted outside the umbrella of the parent Service support infrastructure. Establishment of independent unit identity will provide the most flexible support if a helicopter/tiltrotor aircraft unit is to relocate from ship-to-ship or ship-to-shore. Units should bring as many consumable items as possible.

b. **Funding.** The parent organization of a helicopter/tiltrotor aircraft unit/detachment is responsible for funding the expenses associated with aircraft maintenance and operation. A ship's CO is responsible for funding shipboard operating and maintenance costs from the operating target allowance. Unless specified, funding will be provided by the parent organization or groups performing travel under joint travel regulations. Units required to purchase supplies or fuel from ships' stores will be required to provide appropriate accounting data.

c. **Meals.** Shipboard meals for officers are normally handled by an independent fund to which individual officers contribute. Officers can expect to pay directly or be billed for meals consumed. Enlisted members eat in a dining facility operated by the ship's SUPPO and funded from the ration allowances of the members. Orders for enlisted members should reflect rations in kind for the duration of shipboard embarkation. Coast Guard cutters will treat meals provided to embarked personnel as reimbursable issues and submit Department of Defense (DD) Form-1149, Requisition and Invoice/Shipping Document, IAW COMDTINST M4061.5, *Coast Guard Food Service Manual*.

d. **Supply Requisitions.** The ship's SUPPO can provide assistance in preparing and transmitting properly formatted supply requisitions into the system; however, the embarked helicopter/tiltrotor aircraft unit is responsible for providing the technical, identification, and funding data for the required material.

e. **Cargo Routing.** Procedures for shipping material to units deployed worldwide exist within the Defense Transportation System and are contained in *Defense Transportation Regulation*. The shipper's service control office (SSCO) for all USN units is the Navy Material Transportation Office (NAVMTO) in Norfolk, Virginia. NAVMTO maintains a cargo routing information file (CRIF) that contains up-to-date information on how to route material to covered mobile units. Detachments possessing individual unit identification codes and desiring to avail themselves of this service should make arrangements with NAVMTO and their parent SSCO to be included in the CRIF. The appropriate ships' personnel will keep NAVMTO and other responsible SSCOs apprised of consignment instructions for embarked detachments. Alternatively, material for an embarked detachment may be consigned to the host ship. Detachments operating from Coast Guard cutters should contact the cutter's SUPPO before deployment to coordinate cargo routing.

f. **Aviation Fuel.** If reimbursement is required, embarked helicopter/tiltrotor aircraft units will reimburse ships for aviation fuel at the established DOD price. Selected ships may be capable of processing a DOD fuel identification plate; however, use of a DD Form-1348, *DOD Single Line Item Requisition System Document (Manual)* is more common. For continuing operations, fuel may be billed on the 10th, 20th, and last day of the month to coincide with ship's fuel usage reports. Because many ships are not equipped with meters, aircrew should be prepared to determine the quantity delivered, in pounds, using aircraft fuel gauges.

g. **Hazardous and Flammable Material.** The embarked unit should coordinate all HAZMAT requirements with the ship's SUPPO prior to deployment. The embarked unit is responsible for ensuring their required HAZMAT and corresponding material safety data sheets are requisitioned and loaded. The ability to procure required HAZMAT on deployment is very limited. All HAZMAT must be approved for shipboard use. There is typically limited shipboard storage for HAZMAT aboard all vessels. Stowage and disposal will be IAW current directives provided by the host activity.

h. **Ammunition**

(1) **Parent Service Issuing Activities.** Parent Service ammunition issuing activities will ensure that only authorized and fully serviceable ammunition is issued. Ammunition items issued will be complete as identified by a NSN, DODIC or NALC as well as applicable lot or SNs. Refer to NAVSEA OP 4, *Ammunition and Explosives Safety Afloat,* for further guidance. Ammunition or components without DODICs or NALCs will not be issued to, or embarked on, USN/USCG ships.

(2) **Shipment of Explosives.** Ammunition or other HAZMAT to be shipped to ships by a DOD component or a common (commercial) carrier will be packed, marked, and labeled IAW NAVSEA SW020-AC-SAF-010, *Transportation and Storage Data for Ammunition, Explosives, and Related Hazardous Materials,* and NAVSEA SW020-AG-SAF-010, *Navy Transportation Safety Handbook for Ammunition, Explosives, and Other Related Hazardous Materials,* or appropriate DOD or US Transportation Command HAZMAT regulations for rail, motor vehicle, water, or air shipment.

(3) **Allowance Lists.** Ammunition requirements for units afloat are established to provide a basic authorization by quantity and type to suit the applicable mission and armament of the unit. Normally, these authorizations are in the form of allowance lists.

(4) **Mission Load/Shipfill Ammunition Allowances.** The mission load ammunition allowance is a CNO approved allowance of ammunition carried by aircraft carriers or AASs in support of embarked units such as a CVW or ACE. The shipfill ammunition allowance supports the ship's armament, embarked helicopter/tiltrotor aircraft, and embarked helicopter/tiltrotor aircraft detachments.

(5) **Replenishment.** Embarked helicopter/tiltrotor aircraft ammunition must be replenished by aerial onboard delivery or by pierside onload. Navy ammunition will not be issued to the embarked helicopter/tiltrotor aircraft detachment without the approval of the CNO.

(6) **Army Ordnance Replenishment.** Army A/E packaging has not been tested and approved by the Navy Packaging, Handling, Shipping, and Transportation Center for underway replenishment. Due to this safety risk, all Army A/E will be loaded pierside or transferred aboard as internal aircraft cargo. Army A/E will arrive onboard Navy ships in their standard packaging configurations. When aircraft are used to deliver Army A/E to Navy ships, the aircrew will download the internally loaded A/E, and the host ship will transport the A/E to below deck magazines using ship's armament weapons system equipment.

i. **Mail.** The military postal service is a method for delivery of moderate-sized parts and supplies as well as personal and official mail. Embarked helicopter/tiltrotor aircraft units may obtain a mobile unit Army post office or fleet post office address from the US Military Postal Service Agency, Washington, DC, IAW the DOD 4525.6-M, *Department of Defense Postal Manual.* Establishment of an address and ZIP code is required approximately 60 days in advance. Ships will update mail routing instructions for embarked detachments.

j. **Shipboard Protection.**   Plans should take into account efforts to minimize interruptions to shipboard helicopter/tiltrotor operations that result from an adversary conducting chemical/biological warfare.   See NTTP 3-20.31.470, *Shipboard Biological Warfare/Chemical Warfare Defense and Countermeasures,* and JP 3-11, *Operations in Chemical, Biological, Radiological, and Nuclear (CBRN) Environments.*

# APPENDIX A
## SHIPBOARD HELICOPTER AND TILTROTOR OPERATIONS
## PUBLICATIONS

The following sources of information, procedures, and guidance support shipboard helicopter/tiltrotor operations:

1. **Naval Air Engineering Center-Engineering (NAEC-ENG)-7576,** *Shipboard Aviation Facilities Resume.* This annually updated Navy publication lists every ship with a flight deck and in each case lists aircraft certified to operate on its deck, describes the services available, provides ship's certification levels, and provides a diagram of the flight deck including obstacles. The resume does not provide particulars on the incompatibilities that determine a particular certification level.

> Aviation Facilities Team Lead
> Naval Air Warfare Center Aircraft Division
> Code 4.8.2.5
> Highway 547
> Lakehurst, NJ 08733-5052

For assistance in answering questions relating to shipboard aviation facilities, call the Shipboard Aviation Facility Hotline Action Desk at Defense Switched Network (DSN): 624-2592/Commercial: (732) 323-2592.

2. **Naval Air Training and Operating Procedures Standardization (NATOPS) Manuals.** Distribution of these publications including the USMC MV-22 and USAF CV-22 tiltrotors produced by NAVAIR are established by the automatic distribution requirements list maintained by Naval Air Technical Data and Engineering Service Command, in San Diego, California. For assistance, contact:

> Commanding Officer, Naval Air Technical Data and Engineering Service Command
> Naval Aviation Depot North Island
> Building 90, Code 3.3A
> P.O. Box 357031
> San Diego, CA 92135-7031

These publications can be obtained online at https://mynatec.navair.navy.mil.

a. **NAVAIR 00-80T-105,** *CV NATOPS Manual.* This manual covers pre-deployment training requirements, flight operations, and aircraft handling procedures, ordnance, and deck handling procedures used aboard aircraft carriers.

b. **NAVAIR 00-80T-106,** *LHA/LHD NATOPS Manual.* This manual contains information and procedures for the operation and support of aircraft on and in the vicinity of LHA and LHD class ships.

c. **NAVAIR 00-80T-109,** *Aircraft Refueling NATOPS Manual.* This manual provides technical requirements and operating procedures for ready-issue (retail) aviation fuel operations aboard ship, at shore activities, and in tactical units.

d. **NAVAIR 00-80T-122,** *Helicopter Operating Procedures for Air-Capable Ships NATOPS Manual.* This manual contains information on all aircraft systems, performance data, and operating procedures required for safe and effective operations. The information within this manual is intended to assist staffs, ship COs, squadron COs, helicopter squadron/detachment personnel, and ship personnel in all aspects of effective helicopter operations on ACSs.

3. **COMDTINST M3710.2,** *Shipboard-Helicopter Operational Procedures Manual.* This manual provides the primary source of information for the utilization of the shipboard-helicopter team on all Coast Guard missions. The manual contains specific direction and guidance, and serves as a reference to other pertinent directives and publications. Questions pertaining to this manual should be referred to:

Commandant
United States Coast Guard
Staff Symbol: CG-711
2100 Second Street, SW
Washington, DC 20593-0001
Commercial: (202) 372-2201

4. **FM 1-564,** *Shipboard Operations.* This manual outlines Army procedures for shipboard helicopter operations. The manual is used to coordinate, plan, execute, and teach shipboard operations. Along with Navy publications, it provides information for developing a standardized, progressive program to train crews to proficiency on shipboard operations. The proponent of FM-1-564, *Shipboard Operations,* is Headquarters (HQ) USA Training and Doctrine Command and available from the USA publications agency at http://www.apd.army.mil. User must have an Army knowledge online account to access.

5. **Ordnance Manuals**

Ordnance compatibility information from Commander, NAVSEA:

Commanding Officer, Navy Ordnance Safety and Security Activity
3817 Strauss Avenue
Indian Head, MD 20640-5151
Commercial: (301) 744-6095

Toll-Free "One-Touch" Support for the Fleet: 1-877-4-1-TOUCH or 1-877-418-6824 Distance Support Anchor Desk. This number is exclusively provided for Service members to receive support via a single toll-free number.

a. **NAVSEA OP 4,** *Ammunition and Explosives Safety Afloat.* Contains the minimum safety requirements and regulations for the handling and stowage of A/E as well as related test, assembly, and maintenance. NAVSEA OP 4 also identifies the NAVAIR promulgated Army/Air Force conventional weapons checklists for those weapons and type model series aircraft authorized for shipboard operations.

b. **NAVSEA OP 3565 Volume 2,** *Electromagnetic Radiation Hazards (U) (Hazards to Ordnance).* This manual identifies the RF restrictions and precautions required to be imposed on ordnance designed with EED/EID.

c. **NAVSEA SW020-AC-SAF-010,** *Transportation and Storage Data for Ammunition, Explosives and Related Hazardous Materials.* Includes CNO/WSESRB approved Army/Air Force ordnance packaging and explosive storage data.

6. **Memorandum of Understanding Between The Department of the Navy and The Departments of the Army and The Air Force,** *Army/Air Force Deck Landing Qualification,* **January 2002.** Provides DON, Department of the Army, and Department of the Air Force policy and procedures for Army and Air Force rotorcraft deck landing training and qualification. Available through CNO Air Warfare Division (N98).

7. **Multinational Publications.** Multinational publications are used when supporting NATO and coalition helicopter cross-deck operations. Publications are available by contacting the Navy Warfare Development Command:

Commander
Navy Warfare Development Command
1528 Piersey Street, Building O-27
Norfolk, VA 23511
Commercial: (401) 841-6412
DSN: 948-6412
E-mail: fleetpubs@nwdc.navy.mil

a. **Allied Procedural Publication (APP)-2(F)/Maritime Procedural Publication (MPP) 2(F) Volume I,** *Helicopter Operations From Ships Other Than Aircraft Carriers (HOSTAC) (Maritime VSTOL Data Included).* This manual provides procedures to cross operate safely and efficiently with NATO and coalition partners. This publication contains regional specific guidance as well as national cross-deck procedures.

b. **APP 2(F)/MPP 2(F) Volume II,** *Helicopter Operations From Ships Other Than Aircraft Carriers (HOSTAC) Technical Supplement.* This manual provides technical information on helicopter types and as well as national flight deck information. The data for the US ships is derived directly from the NAEC-ENG-7576, *Shipboard Aviation Facilities Resume.* This publication contains the ship/helicopter interoperability matrix.

   c. **APP 2(F)/MPP 2(F) Volume II, PG,** *Helicopter Operations From Ships Other Than Aircraft Carriers (HOSTAC) Technical Supplement Pocket Guide.* Designed specifically for aircrew, this manual provides national flight deck information.

# APPENDIX B
## SAMPLE FORMATS

Sample formats are included as shown below:

Intentionally Blank

## ANNEX A TO APPENDIX B
### SAMPLE LETTER OF INSTRUCTION

(May be published via message)

3120
Ser

From:   Commander, US (Numbered) Fleet
To:     Commanding Officer, USS _____ (ship)
        Commander, _____ (USA/USAF Aviation unit)

Subj: LETTER OF INSTRUCTION (LOI)

Ref:    (a) [UNDERLINE: EMPLOYMENT SCHEDULE] / Fleet Approval
        (b) JP 3-04, *Joint Shipboard Helicopter Operations*
        (c) MOU between the DON and DOA/DOAF, *Army/Air Force Deck Landing Qualification,* January 2002
        (d) NAVAIR 00-80T-109, *Aircraft Refueling NATOPS Manual*
        (e) MOU among Army/Air Force/Navy/Marine Corps/Coast Guard Safety Centers "Safety Investigation and Reporting of Joint Service Mishaps"

1. Summary. This LOI describes the concept of operations and assigns responsibility for Commanding Officer, USS _____ and assigned detachment from [US Army Command/US Air Force MAJCOM] for DLQ training exercises. This LOI is effective for planning for day/night VFR operations.

2. Mission. USS _____ will provide underway platform services in the conduct of DLQ training exercises (reference (a)). Individual ship routine and exercises may be conducted consistent with attainment of DLQ training goals, safety, and operational security.

3. Concept of Operations. A detachment of helicopters/tiltrotor aircraft from the Army/Air Force will conduct a series of DLQ training exercises consisting of day/night VFR landings on the flight deck, per references (b) through (e).

4. Command Relationships and Responsibilities

   a. Approval to conduct US Army/US Air Force aircraft operations on US Navy and Military Sealift Command ships must be granted by [FLT CDR]. [Numbered Fleet Commander] will initiate the request and inform all units concerned.

   b. Commander, (Numbered Fleet) is the Officer-Scheduling-the-Exercise (OSE).

   c. Commanding Officer, USS _____ is assigned Officer-in-Tactical-Command (OTC) for scheduled DLQ training exercises and will coordinate with area/shore commands for appropriate OPAREA clearances. The host ship can provide limited administrative, logistics, material, maintenance, and repair support. The OTC will ensure a flight deck safety/indoctrination brief is provided to Army/Air Force aircrews prior to the scheduled operations. The OTC will ensure the wind envelopes for the participating aircraft are available to the HCO and the Army/Air Force unit conducting the DLQs.

d. Officer-in-Charge of the [helicopter/tiltrotor aircraft detachment] is assigned as the Officer-Conducting-the-Exercise (OCE) and is directed to conduct vigorous training exercises, pre-exercise training and planning, and to convene a presail conference briefing for major participants. The OCE will ensure prerequisites for shipboard helicopter/tiltrotor aircraft operations are satisfied, will coordinate and supervise training exercises as they pertain to the helicopter/tiltrotor aircraft unit, and will conduct appropriate preflight briefs.

5. Embarked Unit's Shipboard Helicopter/Tiltrotor Operations Prerequisites

a. Training requirements and personnel qualifications to conduct deck landing operations (references (b) and (c)) will be attained prior to actual helicopter/tiltrotor aircraft DLQ training exercises.

b. The helicopter/tiltrotor aircraft detachment will initiate coordination for a DLQ presail conference approximately four weeks prior to the actual operation. A sample DLQ presail conference checklist is provided in reference (c).

c. The helicopter/tiltrotor aircraft detachment should provide a qualified aviation officer onboard ship for liaison between the ship and helicopter aircrews during DLQ.

d. The liaison officer will provide diagrams of pertinent aircraft depicting aircraft egress, fuel cell locations, and TD points for the HCO and crash/fire crew during the DLQ pre-sail conference.

e. Aircrew personnel will brief flight deck/fire party personnel on helicopter/tiltrotor aircraft orientation/safety requirements, which may include a walk-through of the aircraft.

f. The aircraft scheduled for DLQ training should meet the shipboard aviation fuel safety requirements set forth by the Navy (reference (d)). Aircraft shutting down aboard the ship with other than JP5 shall notify the first available ship's controlling authority prior to recovery.

g. Supported units shall be familiar with pertinent shipboard aviation manuals:

(1) NAEC-ENG-7576, *Shipboard Aviation Facilities Resume.*

(2) Sections of NAVAIR 00-80T-122, *Helicopter Operating Procedures for Air-Capable Ships,* pertaining to launch/recovery procedures, ATC, aviation fueling and general helicopter operations.

(3) Sections of NAVAIR 00-80T-106, *LHA/LHD NATOPS Manual,* pertaining to launch/recovery procedures, ATC, aviation fueling and general helicopter operations.

(4) Sections of NAVAIR 00-80T-105, *CV NATOPS Manual,* pertaining to launch/recovery procedures, ATC, aviation fueling and general flight operations.

h. Field deck landing patterns (FDLPs) can be accomplished at any facility that suitably replicates shipboard deck markings. FDLP may also be conducted in approved flight simulators.

6. Administrative/Logistics. The Army/Air Force OCE is responsible for coordinating and arranging shore based administrative and logistics support.

7. Safety Reports. Actions to be taken in the event of aircraft mishap/incident will be per OPNAVINST 3750.6, *The Naval Aviation Safety Program,* and the memorandum of understanding among the Services' safety centers (reference (e)). Initial message notification of aircraft mishap/incident will include as an information addressee, the US Army Headquarters: CSA WASHINGTON DC//DAMOTRI// or US Air Force Headquarters: MAJCOM/CC (Use corresponding MAJCOM's address), as appropriate.

//signed//
Operations Officer
Numbered Fleet Staff

Copy to:
GROUP
SQUADRON
Participating Army/Air Force Unit(s)

Intentionally Blank

# ANNEX B TO APPENDIX B
## SAMPLE CURRENCY WAIVER REQUEST FORMAT

FROM      (Air Force/Army originator)

TO        For Air Force originator (not deployed):
           Respective MAJCOM//A3//
           HQ USAF WASHINGTON DC//XOOS// (Thru appropriate channels)
           For Air Force originator (deployed):
           Respective COMAFFOR or COMAFSOF (Thru appropriate channels)

INFO      NFO US Numbered Fleet (Joint Force Commander)
           HQ USAF Washington DC//A30-AS//
           (Joint Force Navy Component Commander)
           (other appropriate agencies)

(Classification) //N03000//
MSGID/GENADMIN/(ORIGINATING COMMAND)/(OFFICE SYMBOL)//
SUBJ/DECK LANDING QUALIFICATION CURRENCY WAIVER REQUEST//
REF/A/PUB/JOINT PUB 3-04//
AMPN/JOINT SHIPBOARD HELICOPTER OPERATIONS//
1. ( ) IAW REF A, REQUIRE DLQ CURRENCY WAIVER FOR (specify—day/night/NVG) QUALIFICATIONS
2. ( ) QUALIFICATION EXPIRED ON (date) DUE TO (reasons)
3. ( ) NO OTHER OPTIONS TO REQUALIFY EXIST WITHIN CURRENT TIME CONSTRAINTS. (i.e., using USN, USMC, or other Service unit IPs)
4. ( ) FOL INFO PROV:
    A. (name/rank)
    B. TOT HRS (insert #)
    C. TOT NVD HRS (insert #) (if applicable)
    D. TOT SHIP LDNGS (insert #)
    E. TOT NVD SHIP LDNGS (insert #)

Intentionally Blank

# ANNEX C TO APPENDIX B
## SAMPLE WAIVER REQUEST FORMAT

### (For Other than Currency Requirements)

FROM      (Air Force/Army originator)

TO     For Air Force originator (not deployed):
        Respective MAJCOM//A3// (Thru appropriate channels)
        For Air Force originator (deployed):
        Respective COMAFFOR or COMAFSOF (Thru appropriate channels)
        HQ USAF WASHINGTON DC//XOOS// (Thru appropriate channels)
        For Army originator: CSA WASHINGTON DC//DAMO-TRS// (Thru appropriate
           channels)

INFO   US Numbered Fleet
        HQ USAF Washington DC//A30-AS//
        (Joint Force Commander)
        (Joint Force Navy Component Commander)
        (other appropriate agencies)

(Classification) //N03000//
MSGID/GENADMIN/(ORIGINATING COMMAND)/(OFFICE SYMBOL)//
SUBJ/ (specify) WAIVER REQUEST// REF/A/PUB/JOINT PUB 3-04//
AMPN/JOINT SHIPBOARD HELICOPTER OPERATIONS//

RMKS/
1. ( ) (specify waiver requested)
2. ( ) (specify reason for waiver request)
3. ( ) (provide data to support request)

Intentionally Blank

# APPENDIX C
## PRE-DEPLOYMENT PLANNING CHECKLISTS

## 1. General

Cooperation is a key element to all joint operations. It is essential to discuss integration issues prior to conducting joint shipboard helicopter operations. When ship and helicopter/tiltrotor aircraft units are notified about an upcoming shipboard mission, participants should begin coordinating the specifics of their requirements.

## 2. Presail Conference

a. **General.** The naval surface community schedules a presail conference during the early stages of deployment planning involving an embarked unit. The presail conference is an essential part of the compatibility analysis, as it provides key personnel of the participating units with a formal forum to address the concept of upcoming operations at sea as well as procedural and safety issues.

(1) The presail conference normally requires an entire day and should be scheduled no less than six weeks prior to embarkation/deployment. The number and expertise of both embarking unit and ship's company attendees should be sufficient to fully address specific C2, operational, aircraft maintenance, supply/logistics, ordnance, and administrative requirements needed to plan the joint operation. Temporary additional duty/temporary duty funding spent here will significantly enhance preparation, planning, and ultimate success of the joint deployment aboard ship.

(2) Ensure all units involved in the upcoming joint ship helicopter/tiltrotor aircraft operations are invited, paying particular attention to divisional/departmental responsibilities so that representatives can meet their respective counterparts at the conference.

(3) Determine/arrange for a central conference room/area (normally the ship's wardroom aboard the host ship).

(4) Publish a POC/counterpart listing (phone number/e-mail) as early as possible.

(5) Develop agenda and promulgate to all commands/units prior to the conference.

(6) Determine the casualty care response.

(a) Pre-staged medical supplies (blowout kits).

(b) Casualty care training.

(c) Casualty movement to higher capability of care.

(7) The issues in paragraph 2b through 2i should be addressed during the presail conference and/or follow-on discussions/visits between the embarking unit and ship personnel.

b. **Host Ship's Administrative Considerations**

(1) Number, rank, and gender of embarking unit/staffs' officer/enlisted for billeting requirements.

(2) Identify possible administrative, operations/planning, aircraft maintenance workspaces, and ready room locations. (Do a walk-through of these spaces with embarking unit before their representatives depart the ship.)

(3) Identify officer and enlisted mess bill arrangements.

(4) Determine secure space requirements for classified equipment/material stowage.

(5) Determine stowage requirements/security for personal mission equipment (backpacks, special equipment, personal weapons, and computers).

(6) Determine transportation/logistical arrangements of personnel/equipment coming to ship, the cube/weight of equipment to be loaded aboard, the pierside loading required, and the estimated time of arrival of advance equipment.

(7) Develop preliminary embarkation/debarkation load plans with embarking unit to include administrative support items, classified material, and security for same.

(8) Develop computer, local area network, and telephone support requirements for assigned ship's spaces.

(9) Employ information assurance measures to protect and defend the availability, integrity, authentication, confidentiality, and repudiation of the ship's information and information systems.

(10) Arrange for and schedule ship orientation briefing and safety briefing for all embarking personnel immediately upon arrival at ship to include general ship compartment layout/location, general safety aboard ship; and shipboard drills such as GQ, man overboard, fire, and flooding.

(11) Discuss possible augmentation requirements aboard ship (mess duties/laundry/etc.).

c. **Determine health service support requirements.**

d. **Host Ship Flight Operations**

(1) Determine concept of joint operations and mission requirements.

(2) Determine structure of the embarking helicopter/tiltrotor aircraft organization and establish POCs.

(3) Determine number, type, capabilities and operating restrictions (wind launch/recovery limits, blade fold, no rotor brakes, etc.) of helicopter/tiltrotor aircraft to be embarked.

(4) Determine ordnance and fuel requirements for embarking helicopter/tiltrotor aircraft.

(5) Brief ship's communications and navigation equipment. Are embarking unit's communications capabilities compatible with the ship's capabilities?

(6) Brief the air plan development process (with examples of typical day's flight schedule). How is the air plan developed with input from embarking unit/staff?

(7) Discuss ship's overhead message. What does it contain? How does the embarking unit get this message when ashore prior to the fly-aboard?

(8) Establish the requirement for a check-in report—required with ships centerstrike 50 miles out (to inform ship of cargo or personnel to be off-loaded during the fly-aboard).

(9) Determine fly-aboard sequence and download evolution of equipment/personnel/ordnance.

(10) Discuss the following items:

(a) Radio communications interoperability of UHF, very high frequency, secure voice, identification, and friend or foe squawks to include cryptological requirements.

(b) Navigation capabilities (non-TACAN equipped, GPS [Global Positioning System] equipped, etc.) of embarking helicopter/tiltrotor aircraft.

(c) Helicopter/tiltrotor aircraft fuel endurance/standard fuel loads/type fuel (JP4/JP8 status/flash point when flying aboard).

(d) Load-carrying capability (troops/cargo/VERTREP).

(e) Standard ordnance loads/special mission ordnance loads.

(f) Embarking unit pilot shipboard experience and DLQ (day/night) and NVD training requirements.

(g) Briefing requirements needed from host ship (weather, intelligence, radio frequencies, call signs, instrument flight rules [IFR] recovery operations, etc.) for daily operational aircrew briefings.

(h) SAR support requirements needed and assets available (surface and helicopter) to support shipboard helicopter/tiltrotor operations.

(i) Concept of helicopter/tiltrotor aircraft launch cycles, types of ordnance to be carried/employed, ordnance and troop load plan for air plan development. Ensure the ship's ordnance handling officer/combat cargo officer/combat systems officer attend.

(j) Pierside service requirements for both embarkation and debarkation. Pre-deployment troop or equipment loading requirements (both on flight deck fly-aboard and at pierside before ship departs. What pierside services will be needed to accomplish onload/off-load (cranes/forklifts)? How should equipment be packaged (containers, pallets, etc.)?

(k) Mission support equipment requirements (communications and intelligence); compatibility/interoperability of same.

(l) Ready room assignments (visit/inspect spaces).

(m) Flight manuals (operators manual for embarking type helicopter/tiltrotor aircraft provided to host ship (PRIFLY and operations).

e. **Ship's Air Department.** The ship's air department should address the following items:

(1) Air department organizational structure and personnel responsibilities.

(2) Work stations/color codes of flight deck jerseys, general flight deck layout of type/class host ship (dimensions, flight deck lighting [NVD compatible?]), landing spot locations and markings, elevators, ordnance arming spots, location of "bomb farm," location of ordnance elevators, etc.

(3) General flight deck positioning of helicopter/tiltrotor aircraft and support equipment during flight operations (e.g., large helicopter/tiltrotor aircraft aft, medium and light helicopters forward).

(4) General flight deck procedures and safety awareness (FOD, rotorwash, etc.).

(5) PMCFs and general maintenance arrangements POCs.

(6) General time sequence for launch/recovery (aircrew man-up, start engines, etc.).

(7) Sounding of "flight quarters" (what happens?). Discuss "flight quarters for aircraft movement only." Emphasis on plane captains/crew chiefs manning cockpits/brakes for moves and safety when moving aircraft.

(8) FOD walkdown (stress all hands involvement).

(9) Manning cockpits and LSE on launch spot (expected minutes) prior to launch?

(10) Signal to start (LSE or pilot initiated).

(11) Start engines/rotors signal (wind limits for rotor engagement for type helicopter/tiltrotor embarked).

(12) Troop loading. Where will troops be staged? Who escorts the lines of troops ("sticks") to helicopter/tiltrotor aircraft? (Combat cargo coordination required.)

(13) Weapons arming (aviation ordnance loading [including hot/cold tube loading of rockets], arming, de-arming, downloading, and related aircraft maintenance/refueling limitations).

(14) Break down (unchaining of helicopter/tiltrotor aircraft; pilot ready signal: thumbs up to LSE or calls "ready" to boss).

(15) Launching (desired launch sequence, wind-over deck (WOD) requirements for launch).

(16) Departure radio call expected ("fuel to splash and souls onboard?").

(17) In-flight emergencies/IFR recovery procedures.

(18) General landing procedures.

(19) Landing patterns (day/night/NVD).

(20) WOD limits for recovery (general wind envelope).

(21) Aircraft position on spot expected (nose on the "crow's foot?").

(22) WOD limits for helicopter/tiltrotor aircraft rotor shutdown and blade fold?

(23) Embarked helicopters with rotor brakes. Which do not have rotor brakes?

(24) Special aircraft handling equipment requirements. Is the embarking unit bringing these items aboard?

(25)  Helicopter/tiltrotor aircraft TD procedures (TD points).  Who has TD chains? Embarked unit brings?

(26)  Ordnance de-arm/hung ordnance procedures and hung ordnance flight pattern.

(27)  Crash/salvage procedures and required lift slings for non-Navy helicopter/tiltrotor aircraft.

(28)  Integrity watch/aircraft security requirements and responsibilities.

f. **Discussion Points for Embarking Unit**

(1)  What is embarking unit's organizational structure and who are ship's POCs?

(2)  Who is embarked unit's designated flight deck maintenance representative/liaison contact for air department?

(3)  Are there unique aircraft handling characteristics and handling equipment required for specific types of helicopter/tiltrotor aircraft to be embarked (tiller/guide bar for H-47, handling wheels for skid type, etc.) to be addressed to air department?

(4)  Who supplies what support equipment (GSE, TD chains)?

(5)  Fueling ports and TD points known to host ship air department?

(6)  Type of fuel available on host ship?  JP5?

(7)  Are alternative fueling procedures (gravity refueling) and equipment (Wiggins fitting) available for refueling?

(8)  What type of shipboard defueling capability exists?  Is it compatible with your helicopter/tiltrotor aircraft?

(9)  What helicopter/tiltrotor aircraft heavy weather TD equipment (blade TDs, blade supports, etc.) are needed for heavy weather/high winds for flight deck (45 knots plus)?

(10)  Does air department know type helicopter/tiltrotor aircraft pilot/crew positions, type helicopter/tiltrotor aircraft rescue procedures, engine shutdown levers, battery location, ordnance locations/type ordnance? (Termed "crash and smash brief"; normally done immediately after fly-aboard.)

(11)  Does embarking helicopter/tiltrotor aircraft have a maximum (never exceed) fuel pressure limitation (ship fueling station normally fuels at 55 psi)?  Is ship's fueling system compatible (fuel nozzle, fuel pressure, defueling system)?

(12) Has all ordnance that requires loading onto the host ship to meet the mission assignment been identified and preapproved by the WSESRB prior to ammunition onload? When and where will the ammunition be onloaded? Where should the ammunition be shipped to for follow-on load on the host ship?

(13) Does ship's flight deck have NVD compatible lighting and qualified LSEs to accomplish NVD operations?

(14) How will the weapons department be advised of air plan aviation ordnance requirements? Where will aviation ordnance be staged on the flight deck? How much staging lead time can be provided to facilitate aircraft loading? Where will expendable countermeasures be pre-loaded? What procedures must be followed for rocket cold/hot tube loading? What ammunition accountability procedures will be utilized?

g. **Shipboard Aircraft Maintenance**

(1) What are the aircraft maintenance capabilities of the host ship?

(2) Does it have an AIMD (to accomplish higher than squadron/company level maintenance)?

(3) Does this type/class ship normally operate similar type helicopter/tiltrotor aircraft?

(4) Does host ship's supply department stock aviation supplies (AVCAL)? These supplies (also listed by NSN) can be compared to your deployment needs. An embarking supply representative must verify this at the planning conference and before deployment. (Note: This AVCAL may change prior to deployment due to air wing and type aircraft fleet needs.)

(5) What special technical test equipment is needed to support your helicopter/tiltrotor aircraft (electronic test equipment, ordnance equipment particular to type helicopter/tiltrotor aircraft, etc.) that will not be found aboard ship?

(6) Where will the embarking unit safely stow the myriad equipment to be either self-lifted to the ship or loaded aboard at the pier?

(7) Where are the embarking unit's assigned maintenance spaces aboard ship? (Take the time to look at these spaces before you leave the ship while on your visit.)

(8) What department/individual needs to know if heavy/critical maintenance is to be performed? (Example: The raising of aircraft up on jack stands to facilitate maintenance should be relayed to the ship's OOD so that precautions are in place to prevent any sharp maneuvering of the ship while the helicopter/tiltrotor aircraft is on jack stands.)

(9) Who does the embarking unit coordinate with to perform an aircraft wash evolution aboard ship? Aircraft deployed at sea need protection from the salt-laden environment. This requires frequent fresh water washes.

(10) Does the embarking unit have the correct TD chains for deployment (Navy TD-1A chains)? If not, where does the unit get them?

(11) Were the embarked unit personnel working on the flight deck thoroughly briefed on the use of flight deck/hangar deck fire fighting equipment?

(12) How do the embarking unit's lines of supply/logistics integrate with the Navy's supply/logistics system?

(13) Is host ship's electrical power and GSE support compatible with embarking unit aircraft (voltage/phase/hydraulic fittings)?

(14) What TD supplies (cargo straps, etc.) does the embarking unit have to ensure safe TD of all embarked equipment/boxes at sea?

h. **Flight Deck/Hangar Operations**

(1) Ordnance.

(2) Required ordnance safety briefings.

(3) Ordnance crew certification requirements (embarked unit and host ship).

(4) A comprehensive listing of all types/classes of ordnance (aircraft and personal weapons) by NSN and DODIC proposed for embarkation aboard ship.

(5) Required ordnance packaging and marking for shipment and onload aboard ship.

(6) Schedule and method of ordnance onload (pierside or fly-aboard).

(7) Designated ordnance stowage areas aboard ship for joint ordnance.

(8) Temporary stowage areas for ordnance/ammunition on the flight deck and prevention of FOD.

(9) Stowage, point of issue, responsibility for the issue, and accountability of personal weapons and ammunition aboard ship.

(10) Ship's HERO restrictions for specified ordnance. Who (in ship's company) is responsible for setting HERO?

(11) Ordnance load plan input for ship's notional air plan.

(12) Aviation ordnance storage, buildup, loading and unloading procedures aboard ship (see NAVAIR 00-80T-106, *LHA/LHD NATOPS Manual,* NAVAIR-00-08T-105, *CV NATOPS Manual, and* NAVAIR 00-80T-122 *(NATOPS), Helicopter Operating Procedures for Air Capable Ships.*)

(13) Aviation crew-served weapons on the flight deck (type and safety).

(14) Positioning of aircraft with forward-firing ordnance (rockets) on flight deck.

(15) Hung ordnance procedures (flight patterns and download).

(16) Post mission/debarkation ordnance off-load requirements.

   i. **Safety**

(1) Schedule general shipboard safety brief for embarking unit/staff.

(2) Schedule flight deck safety orientation and flight crew rescue brief for air department.

(3) Review aircraft mishap reporting responsibilities. Ensure availability of ships pre-accident and embarking unit pre-accident plans.

(4) Review proper equipment for flight deck.

(5) Explain flight deck FOD program.

Intentionally Blank

# ANNEX A TO APPENDIX C
## DECK LANDING QUALIFICATION PRESAIL CHECKLIST

The following DLQ checklist has been extracted from MOU between the DON and the Department of the Army and the Department of the Air Force, *Army/Air Force Deck Landing Qualification,* January 2002.

1. Create key personnel list:

| | Duty Position | POC | Phone/E-mail |
|---|---|---|---|
| Aviation | _____ | _____ | _____ |
| Ship | _____ | _____ | _____ |

2. Establish:

    a. DLQ date _____

    b. Schedule _____

    c. Ship location _____

3. Field DLQ requirements (as required) _____

4. Type and number of aircraft involved _____

5. DLQ requirements _____

    a. Number of pilots _____

    b. Number of landings (D/N/NVD) _____

6. Surface/air clearances (ship responsibility) _____

7. Aviation facility waiver (if required) _____

8. Communications/NAVAIDS/transmitters _____

    a. Ship call sign and frequencies (primary and alternate) _____

    b. Aircraft call sign _____

    c. Ship emitter restrictions (EMV/HIRTA) _____

9. Ship overhead message (include PLAD message address) _____

10. Safety/operations brief (ship responsibility) _____

11. Crash rescue procedures _____

12. SAR/lost plane procedures _____

13. Ship certification (level/class/type) and support _____

    a. Landings/spotting restrictions _____

    b. Maintenance capability (fresh water rinse) _____

14. Launch/recovery envelopes _____

    a. Wind _____

    b. Pitch/roll _____

15. Rotor engage/disengage and limits _____

16. Rotor brake equipped? _____

17. Weather procedures _____

    a. Minimums (D/N/NVD) _____

    b. Inadvertent IMC _____

18. Fuel requirements onboard ship _____

    a. JP5 considerations _____

    b. NATO D1 or Wiggins fitting _____

19. Fuel cost reimbursement _____

20. Flight liaison officer _____

    a. Embarkation/debarkation _____

    b. Berthing/messing _____

    c. Passenger/maintenance transfer (prohibited at night) _____

21. Shore-based administrative logistics _____

a. Coordinator _____

b. Transient A/C local operations brief (base operations) _____

c. Helicopter ramp parking _____

d. Fresh water wash _____

e. Billeting _____

f. Messing _____

g. Local transportation _____

Numbered Fleet Air Operations POCs:

CTF-20 Air Operations (Atlantic)
DSN: (757) 836-2514
Commercial: (757) 836-2514

COMTHIRDFLT (Eastern Pacific)
DSN: (312) 577-4241
Commercial: (619) 767-4241

COMFOURFLT
DSN: (312) 960-6914
Commercial: (904) 270-6914

COMFIFTHFLT (USCENTCOM AOR)
DSN: (318) 439-4132
Commercial: 011-973-1785-4132

COMSIXTHFLT (USEUCOM, USAFRICOM AOR)
DSN: (314) 626-4551
Commercial: 011-39-081-568-4551

COMSEVENTHFLT (Western Pacific/IO)
DSN: (315) 243-7719
Commercial: 011-81-46-816-7719

COMUSNAVSOUTH (USSOUTHCOM AOR)
DSN: 831-3676
Commercial: (787) 865-3676

Intentionally Blank

## ANNEX B TO APPENDIX C
## EMBARKED UNIT PRE-DEPLOYMENT PLANNING CHECKLIST

1. Security clearance message/FAX: _____

2. Helicopter/tiltrotor aircraft detachment certification: _____

3. Requirements for aviators

    a. Initial qualification and currency requirements: _____

        (1) DLQ LOI: _____

        (2) Security clearance: _____

    b. Aviators should attend an instrument refresher training course: _____

    c. Overwater training requirements: _____

    d. Overwater gunnery training: _____

    e. NVD training: _____

    f. Nonstandard aviation maneuver training: _____

    g. Underwater egress training: _____

    h. Helicopter Emergency Egress Device System [HEEDS] training: _____

    i. Anti-exposure suits/cold weather gear: _____

4. Requirements message, classified material stowage/handling: _____

5. Alpha/manning roster, embarked unit manning roster: _____

6. Helicopter/tiltrotor aircraft specifications (i.e., diagrams)

    a. Aircraft egress: _____

    b. Refueling locations and grounding points: _____

    c. TD points: _____

    d. Desired wind envelopes: _____

    e.  Pitch and roll limitations: _____

    f.  Servicing locations (i.e., hydraulic, pneumatic): _____

7.  Pre-exercise planning

    a.  Host squadron/hangaring of aircraft: _____

    b.  CCR/Wiggins capability: _____

    c.  Flash point minimums for hangaring of aircraft: _____

    d.  Ordnance delivery and handling: _____

    e.  NVD currency, requirements, and capabilities: _____

    f.  Emergency low visibility approach [ELVA] currency and training: _____

    g.  Blade folding capability and heavy weather planning: _____

    h.  Flight quarters versus flight hours: _____

8.  Communications

    a.  Ship communications (i.e., walkie-talkie, mickey mouse ears): _____

    b.  Available/clouded frequencies: _____

    c.  EMCON procedures: _____

    d.  RF interference: _____

9.  Service and maintenance requirements

    a.  Corrosion prevention and control: _____

    b.  POL requirements: _____

    c.  General and special maintenance requirements: _____

    d.  GSE: _____

    e.  Aviation life support equipment (ALSE) inspection/certification: _____

10.  Aircraft movement, respotting, and securing requirements

a. Blade fold/removal capability and requirements (support equipment): _____

b. Blade securing requirements: _____

c. Tow bar/spotting dolly compatibility: _____

d. Initial, permanent, heavy weather securing requirements: _____

11. Detachment/aircraft space assignments

a. Proper identification of tac numbers of assigned spaces: _____

b. Electrical power requirements: _____

12. Requirements for aviation detachment personnel assigned to flight deck duties

a. Personal protective clothing and equipment (cranial, steel-toe boots, hearing/eye protection: _____

b. Flight deck clothing color coding: _____

c. Shipboard fire fighting indoctrination training is required: _____

d. NVG compatible flashlights: _____

13. Corrosion prevention and control

a. Fresh water rinse: _____

b. Saltwater encrustation: _____

c. Passenger/maintenance transfer (prohibited at night) _____

14. Aircraft departure and recovery procedures

a. Deck status lights: _____

b. Aircraft handling signals: _____

c. Command and display signals: _____

d. Communications: _____

e. NVD operations: _____

f.  ATC procedures: _____

g.  Takeoff and recovery minimums: _____

h.  Standard landing patterns and zones: _____

i.  IFR (instrument landing aids): _____

j.  Visual landing aids: _____

k.  EMCON: _____

l.  TACAN/radio frequencies: _____

m.  Control areas and approach charts: _____

n.  Wind envelopes: _____

o.  Brevity codes: _____

15.  General fueling procedures

a.  Type of fuel: _____

b.  Preferred procedures: _____

c.  Alternate methods: _____

d.  Hot refueling: _____

e.  NATO 01 or Wiggins nozzles: _____

f.  Grounding/bonding: _____

16.  Aviation ordnance

a.  Movement, handling, and stowage of explosive ordnance: _____

b.  Weapons staging: _____

c.  Weapons assembly and disassembly: _____

d.  Weapons loading and downloading: _____

e.  Weapons arming and disarming: _____

f. WSESRB: _____

g. Adherence to NAVSEA OP 4, *Ammunition and Explosives Safety Afloat*: _____

h. Establish HERO and/or EMCON bill: _____

i. Personnel qualification and certification: _____

j. Emergency procedures: _____

17. Safety

a. General safety measures: _____

b. Flight deck clothing and equipment: _____

c. Passengers: _____

d. FOD: _____

e. Helicopter/tiltrotor aircraft equipment hazards: _____

f. Weapon hazards: _____

g. Aircraft movement and respotting: _____

h. Helicopter/tiltrotor aircraft fire party: _____

i. Emergency procedures: _____

18. Aircraft maintenance

a. GSE: _____

b. Compatible POL and associated fuels: _____

c. Special tools: _____

d. Inspections: _____

e. Pack-up load plans: _____

f. HAZMAT: _____

19. Logistics

    a.  Shipboard orientation: _____

    b.  Funding: _____

    c.  Meals: _____

    d.  Berthing (male/female): _____

    e.  Watch bill requirements: _____

    f.  Supply: _____

    g.  Cargo routing: _____

    h.  Aviation fuel: _____

    i.  Hazardous and flammable material: _____

    j.  Personal weapons: _____

    k.  Ammunition: _____

    l.  Mail: _____

    m.  Navy customs and courtesies: _____

    n.  Publications: _____

    o.  ALSE: _____

    p.  SAR: _____

    q.  GQ/man overboard: _____

# APPENDIX D
## REFERENCES

The development of JP 3-04 is based upon the following primary references:

## 1. General

a. Title 46, Code of Federal Regulations, *Shipping.*

b. MIL-STD 464A, *Department of Defense Interface Standard: Electromagnetic Environmental Effects Requirements for Systems.*

## 2. Department of Defense Publications

DOD Manual 6055.09-M, *DOD Ammunition and Explosive Safety Standards.*

## 3. Chairman of the Joint Chiefs of Staff Publications

a. Chairman of the Joint Chiefs of Staff Instruction 5120.02, *Joint Doctrine Development System.*

b. Chairman of the Joint Chiefs of Staff Manual 5120.01, *Joint Doctrine Development Process.*

c. JP 1-02, *DOD Dictionary of Military and Associated Terms.*

d. JP 3-0, *Joint Operations.*

e. JP 3-02.1, *Amphibious Embarkation and Debarkation.*

## 4. United States Transportation Command Publications

*Defense Transportation Regulation.*

## 5. Multi-Service Publications

a. FM 1-02.1/MCRP 3-25B/NTTP 6-02.1/AFTTP(I) 3-2.5, *Multi-Service Brevity Codes.*

b. OPNAVINST 8020.14/Marine Corps Order P8020.11, *Department of the Navy Explosives Safety Policy.*

## 6. North Atlantic Treaty Organization Publications

a. APP 2(F)/MPP 2(F) Volume I, *Helicopter Operations From Ships Other Than Aircraft Carriers (HOSTAC) (Maritime VSTOL Data Included).*

b. APP 2(F)/MPP 2(F) Volume II, *Helicopter Operations From Ships Other Than Aircraft Carriers (HOSTAC) Technical Supplement.*

c. APP 2(F)/MPP 2(F) Volume II PG, *Helicopter Operations From Ships Other Than Aircraft Carriers (HOSTAC) Technical Supplement Pocket Guide.*

d. ATP-17, *Naval Arctic Manual.*

## 7. United States Ordnance Publications

a. NAVSEA OP 4, *Ammunition and Explosives Safety Afloat.*

b. NAVSEA OP 3565/NAVAIR 16-1-529, Volume 2, *Electromagnetic Radiation Hazards (U) (Hazards to Ordnance).*

c. NAVSEA S9086-VG-STM-000, *Naval Ships Technical Manual.*

d. NAVSEA S9522-AA-HBK-010, *Description, Operation, and Instruction Book Magazine Sprinkler System.*

e. NAVSEA SW010-AF-ORD-010, *Identification of Ammunition.*

f. NAVSEA SW020-AC-SAF-010, SW020-AC-SAF-020, and SW020-AC-SAF-030, *Transportation and Storage Data for Ammunition, Explosives, and Related Hazardous Materials.*

g. NAVSEA SW020-AG-SAF-010, *Navy Transportation Safety Handbook for Ammunition, Explosives, and Other Related Hazardous Materials.*

h. NAVSEA SW050-AB-MMA-010, *Pyrotechnic Screening and Marking Items.*

i. NAVSEA SW050-AC-ORD-010/NA-11-15-8, *Toxic Hazard Associated with Pyrotechnic Devices.*

j. NAVSEA SW060-AA-MMA-010, *Demolition Material.*

k. NAVAIR 11-1F-2, *Description and Characteristics Airborne Bomb and Rocket Fuze Manual.*

l. NAVAIR 11-140-12, *Airborne Weapons Assembly Manual Aircraft Rocket Systems 2.75-Inch And 5.0-Inch Organizational, Intermediate and Depot Maintenance Activities.*

m. NAVAIR 11-140-12-3, *Airborne Weapons Assembly Checklist Organizational and Intermediate Rocket Launcher Testing Procedures.*

n. NAVAIR 19-15BC-12, *Operation and Intermediate Maintenance Instructions with Illustrated Parts Breakdown Bomb Skid Assembly AERO-12C.*

o. NAVAIR 00-80R-14, *NATOPS US Navy Aircraft Firefighting and Rescue Manual.*

## 8. Service Publications

a. FM-1-564, *Shipboard Operations.*

b. MCRP 4-11.3G, *Unit Embarkation Handbook.*

c. COMDTINST M3710.1, *Coast Guard Air Operations Manual.*

d. COMDTINST M3710.2, *Shipboard-Helicopter Operational Procedures Manual.*

e. NAVAIR 00-80T-105, *CV NATOPS Manual.*

f. NAVAIR 00-80T-106, *LHA/LHD NATOPS Manual.*

g. NAVAIR 00-80T-109, *NATOPS Aircraft Refueling Manual.*

h. NAVAIR 00-80T-120, *CVN Flight/Hangar Deck NATOPS Manual.*

i. NAVAIR 00-80T-122, *Helicopter Operating Procedures for Air-Capable Ships NATOPS Manual.*

j. NAVAIR A1-V22AB-NFM-000, *NATOPS Flight Manual Navy Model MV-22B Tiltrotor.*

k. NAVAIR A1-V22AC-AFM-000, *NATOPS Flight Manual USAF Series CV-22 Tiltrotor.*

l. NAEC-ENG-7576, *Shipboard Aviation Facilities Resume.*

m. Naval Safety Center Instruction 8020.1, *Ship/Submarine Explosives Safety Surveys and Checklist.*

n. NAVSEAINST 8020.7D, *Hazards of Electromagnetic Radiation to Ordnance Safety Program.*

o. NAVSUP P-724, *Conventional Ordnance Stockpile Management.*

p. NAVSUP P-801, *Notice of Ammunition Reclassification (NAR) Manual.*

q. NAVSUP P-802, *Navy Ammunition Logistics Codes.*

r. OPNAVINST 3710.7U, *NATOPS General Flight and Operating Instructions.*

s. OPNAVINST 8023.24, *Navy Personnel Ammunition and Explosives Handling Qualification and Certification Program.*

t. OPNAVINST 5100.19, *Navy Safety Precautions for Forces Afloat.*

u. OPNAVINST 5530.1, *Department of the Navy Physical Security Instruction for Sensitive Conventional Arms, Ammunition, and Explosives (AA&E).*

v. OPNAVINST 5720.2, *Embarkation of US Naval Ships.*

# APPENDIX E
## ADMINISTRATIVE INSTRUCTIONS

### 1. User Comments

Users in the field are highly encouraged to submit comments on this publication to: Deputy Director, Joint Staff J-7, Joint and Coalition Warfighting, 116 Lake View Parkway, Suffolk, VA 23435-2697. These comments should address content (accuracy, usefulness, consistency, and organization), writing, and appearance.

### 2. Authorship

The lead agent for this publication is the US Navy. The Joint Staff doctrine sponsor for this publication is the Director for Operational Plans and Interoperability (J-7).

### 3. Supersession

This publication supersedes JP 3-04, *Joint Shipboard Helicopter Operations,* 30 September 2008.

### 4. Change Recommendations

    a. Recommendations for urgent changes to this publication should be submitted:

        INFO: JOINT STAFF WASHINGTON DC//J7-JEDD//
        JOINT STAFF WASHINGTON DC//J3//

    b. Routine changes should be submitted electronically to the Deputy Director, Joint and Coalition Warfighting, Joint and Coalition Warfighting Center, Joint Doctrine Support Division and info the lead agent and the Director for Joint Force Development, J7/JEDD.

    c. When a Joint Staff directorate submits a proposal to the Chairman of the Joint Chiefs of Staff that would change source document information reflected in this publication, that directorate will include a proposed change to this publication as an enclosure to its proposal. The Services and other organizations are requested to notify the Joint Staff/J-7 when changes to source documents reflected in this publication are initiated.

### 5. Distribution

Local reproduction is authorized and access to unclassified publications is unrestricted. However, access to and reproduction authorization for classified JPs must be IAW DOD Manual 5200.01, *DOD Information Security Program: Overview, Classification, and Declassification.*

## 6. Distribution of Electronic Publications

a. Joint Staff J-7 will not print copies of JPs for distribution. Electronic versions are available on the Joint Doctrine, Education, and Training Electronic Information System Web site at https://jdeis.js.mil/jdeis/index.jsp (NIPRNET), and http://jdeis.js.smil.mil (SIPRNET), and on the Joint Electronic Library (JEL) at http://www.dtic.mil/doctrine (NIPRNET).

b. Only approved JPs and joint test publications are releasable outside the combatant commands, Services, and Joint Staff. Release of any classified JP to foreign governments or foreign nationals must be requested through the local embassy (Defense Attaché Office) to DIA, Defense Foreign Liaison/IE-3, 200 MacDill Blvd., Joint Base Anacostia-Bolling, Washington, DC 20340-5100.

c. JEL CD-ROM. Upon request of a JDDC member, the Joint Staff J-7 will produce and deliver one CD-ROM with current JPs. This JEL CD-ROM will be updated not less than semi-annually and when received can be locally reproduced for use within the combatant commands and Services.

# GLOSSARY
## PART I—ACRONYMS AND ABBREVIATIONS

| | |
|---|---|
| AAS | amphibious assault ship |
| AATCC | amphibious air traffic control center |
| ACE | aviation combat element (USMC) |
| ACS | air-capable ship |
| A/E | ammunition/explosives |
| AFTTP(I) | Air Force tactics, techniques, and procedures (instruction) |
| AIMD | aircraft intermediate maintenance department |
| ALN | ammunition lot number |
| ALSE | aviation life support equipment |
| APP | allied procedural publication |
| ARG | amphibious ready group |
| ASP | ammunition supply point |
| ATC | air traffic control |
| ATP | allied tactical publication |
| AVCAL | aviation consolidated allowance list |
| | |
| C | Celsius |
| C2 | command and control |
| CCR | closed circuit refueling |
| CNO | Chief of Naval Operations |
| CO | commanding officer |
| COMDTINST | Commandant, United States Coast Guard, instruction |
| COMUSFLTFORCOM | Commander, United States Fleet Forces Command |
| COMUSPACFLT | Commander, United States Pacific Fleet |
| CRIF | cargo routing information file |
| CV | aircraft carrier |
| CVN | aircraft carrier, nuclear |
| CVW | carrier air wing |
| | |
| DD | Department of Defense form |
| DLQ | deck landing qualification |
| DMHS | Defense Message Handling System |
| DOD | Department of Defense |
| DODIC | Department of Defense identification code |
| DON | Department of the Navy |
| DSN | Defense Switched Network |
| | |
| E3 | electromagnetic environmental effects |
| EED | electro-explosive device |
| EID | electrically initiated device |
| EM | electromagnetic |
| EMCON | emission control |
| EME | electromagnetic environment |

| | |
|---|---|
| EMI | electromagnetic interference |
| EMV | electromagnetic vulnerability |
| EWO | electronic warfare officer |
| | |
| F | Fahrenheit |
| FM | field manual (Army) |
| FOD | foreign object damage |
| | |
| GCC | geographic combatant commander |
| GQ | general quarters |
| GSE | ground support equipment |
| | |
| HAZMAT | hazardous materials |
| HCO | helicopter control officer |
| HDC | helicopter direction center |
| HERF | hazards of electromagnetic radiation to fuels |
| HERO | hazards of electromagnetic radiation to ordnance |
| HERP | hazards of electromagnetic radiation to personnel |
| HIFR | helicopter in-flight refueling |
| HIRTA | high intensity radio transmission area |
| HQ | headquarters |
| | |
| IAW | in accordance with |
| IFR | instrument flight rules |
| IMC | instrument meteorological conditions |
| IMRL | individual material requirements list |
| ISO | International Organization for Standardization |
| | |
| JFC | joint force commander |
| JOERAD | joint spectrum center ordnance electromagnetic environmental effects risk assessment database |
| JP | joint publication |
| JP4 | jet propulsion fuel, type 4 |
| JP5 | jet propulsion fuel, type 5 |
| JP8 | jet propulsion fuel, type 8 |
| JSC | Joint Spectrum Center |
| | |
| lb | pound |
| LHA | amphibious assault ship (general purpose) |
| LHD | amphibious assault ship (multipurpose) |
| LSE | landing signalman enlisted |
| LSO | landing signals officer |
| | |
| MCRP | Marine Corps reference publication |
| MGW | maximum gross weight |
| MHE | materials handling equipment |

| | |
|---|---|
| MIL-STD | military standard |
| MOU | memorandum of understanding |
| MPP | maritime procedural publication |
| | |
| NAEC-ENG | Naval Air Engineering Center–Engineering |
| NALC | Navy ammunition logistics code |
| NAR | notice of ammunition reclassification |
| NATO | North Atlantic Treaty Organization |
| NATOPS | Naval Air Training and Operating Procedures Standardization |
| NAVAIDS | navigational aids |
| NAVAIR | Naval Air Systems Command |
| NAVMTO | Navy Material Transportation Office |
| NAVSEA | Naval Sea Systems Command |
| NAVSEAINST | Naval Sea Systems Command instruction |
| NAVSUP | Naval Supply Systems Command |
| NAWCAD | Naval Air Warfare Center, Aircraft Division |
| NOLSC | Naval Operational Logistics Support Center |
| NOSSA | Navy Ordnance Safety and Security Activity |
| NSN | national stock number |
| NSWCDD | Naval Surface Warfare Center Dahlgren Division |
| NTTP | Navy tactics, techniques, and procedures |
| NVD | night vision device |
| | |
| 1MC | general announcing system |
| OIC | officer in charge |
| OOD | officer of the deck |
| OP | ordnance publication |
| OPNAVINST | Chief of Naval Operations instruction |
| | |
| P | publication |
| PLAD | plain language address directory |
| PMCF | post maintenance check flight |
| POC | point of contact |
| POD | plan of the day |
| POE | port of embarkation |
| POL | petroleum, oils, and lubricants |
| PRIFLY | primary flight control |
| psi | pounds per square inch |
| | |
| RF | radio frequency |
| RPM | revolutions per minute |
| | |
| SAR | search and rescue |
| SN | serial number |
| SOF | special operations forces |

| | |
|---|---|
| SOP | standard operating procedure |
| SSCO | shipper's service control office |
| SUPPO | supply officer |
| | |
| TACAN | tactical air navigation |
| TD | tie down |
| T/M/S | type, model, and/or series |
| TYCOM | type commander |
| | |
| UAS | unmanned aircraft system |
| UHF | ultrahigh frequency |
| USA | United States Army |
| USAF | United States Air Force |
| USCG | United States Coast Guard |
| USMC | United States Marine Corps |
| USN | United States Navy |
| | |
| VERTREP | vertical replenishment |
| VMC | visual meteorological conditions |
| VTOL-UAS | vertical takeoff and landing unmanned aircraft system |
| | |
| WOD | wind-over deck |
| WSESRB | Weapon System Explosive Safety Review Board |
| | |
| XO | executive officer |

**air-capable ship.** A ship other than an aircraft carrier, nuclear; amphibious assault ship (general purpose); or amphibious assault ship (multipurpose) from which aircraft can take off, be recovered, or routinely receive and transfer logistic support. Also called **ACS.** (Approved for incorporation into JP 1-02.)

**aircraft tiedown.** None. (Approved for removal from JP 1-02.)

**ammunition lot.** A quantity of homogeneous ammunition, identified by a unique lot number, which is manufactured, assembled, or renovated by one producer under uniform conditions and which is expected to function in a uniform manner. (JP 1-02. SOURCE: JP 3-04)

**amphibious assault ship (general purpose).** None. (Approved for removal from JP 1-02.)

**amphibious aviation assault ship.** None. (Approved for removal from JP 1-02.)

**arm or de-arm.** None. (Approved for removal from JP 1-02.)

**aviation ship.** None. (Approved for removal from JP 1-02.)

**bill.** A ship's publication listing operational or administrative procedures. (JP 1-02. SOURCE: JP 3-04)

**cartridge-actuated device.** Small explosive devices used to eject stores from launched devices, actuate other explosive systems, or provide initiation for aircrew escape devices. Also called **CAD.** (Approved for replacement of "cartridge actuated device" in JP 1-02.)

**combat information center.** The agency in a ship or aircraft manned and equipped to collect, display, evaluate, and disseminate tactical information for the use of the embarked flag officer, commanding officer, and certain control agencies. Also called **CIC.** (JP 1-02. SOURCE: JP 3-04)

**control area.** A controlled airspace extending upwards from a specified limit above the Earth. (JP 1-02. SOURCE: JP 3-04)

**de-arming.** An operation in which a weapon is changed from a state of readiness for initiation to a safe condition. Also called **safing.** (JP 1-02. SOURCE: JP 3-04)

**deck status light.** A three-colored light (red, amber, green) controlled from the primary flight control. Navy—The light displays the status of the ship to support flight operations. United States Coast Guard—The light displays clearance for a helicopter to conduct a given evolution. (JP 1-02. SOURCE: JP 3-04)

**delaying action.** None. (Approved for removal from JP 1-02.)

**delaying operation.** An operation in which a force under pressure trades space for time by slowing down the enemy's momentum and inflicting maximum damage on the enemy without, in principle, becoming decisively engaged. (JP 1-02. SOURCE: JP 3-04)

**downloading.** An operation that removes airborne weapons or stores from an aircraft. (JP 1-02. SOURCE: JP 3-04)

**electro-explosive device.** An explosive or pyrotechnic component that initiates an explosive, burning, electrical, or mechanical train and is activated by the application of electrical energy. Also called **EED.** (JP 1-02. SOURCE: JP 3-04)

**flight deck.** 1. In certain airplanes, an elevated compartment occupied by the crew for operating the airplane in flight. 2. The upper deck of an aircraft carrier that serves as a runway. The deck of an air-capable ship, amphibious aviation assault ship, or aircraft carrier used to launch and recover aircraft. (Approved for incorporation into JP 1-02.)

**flight deck officer.** Officer responsible for the safe movement of aircraft on or about the flight deck of an aviation-capable ship. Also called **FDO.** (JP 1-02. SOURCE: JP 3-04)

**flight quarters.** A ship configuration that assigns and stations personnel at critical positions to conduct safe flight operations. (JP 1-02. SOURCE: JP 3-04)

**foreign object damage.** Rags, pieces of paper, line, articles of clothing, nuts, bolts, or tools that, when misplaced or caught by air currents normally found around aircraft operations (jet blast, rotor or prop wash, engine intake), cause damage to aircraft systems or weapons or injury to personnel. Also called **FOD.** (JP 1-02. SOURCE: JP 3-04)

**handling (ordnance).** None. (Approved for removal from JP 1-02.)

**hazards of electromagnetic radiation to fuels.** The potential hazard that is created when volatile combustibles, such as fuel, are exposed to electromagnetic fields of sufficient energy to cause ignition. Also called **HERF.** (JP 1-02. SOURCE: JP 3-04)

**hazards of electromagnetic radiation to ordnance.** The danger of accidental actuation of electro-explosive devices or otherwise electrically activating ordnance because of radio frequency electromagnetic fields. Also called **HERO.** (Approved for incorporation into JP 1-02.)

**hazards of electromagnetic radiation to personnel.** The potential hazard that exists when personnel are exposed to an electromagnetic field of sufficient intensity to heat the human body. Also called **HERP.** (JP 1-02. SOURCE: JP 3-04)

**helicopter landing zone.** None. (Approved for removal from JP 1-02.)

**HERO SAFE ordnance.** Any ordnance item that is percussion initiated, sufficiently shielded or otherwise so protected that all electro-explosive devices contained by the item are immune to adverse effects (safety or reliability) when the item is employed in its expected radio frequency environments, provided that the general hazards of electromagnetic radiation to ordnance requirements defined in the hazards from electromagnetic radiation manual are observed. (JP 1-02. SOURCE: JP 3-04)

**HERO SUSCEPTIBLE ordnance.** Any ordnance item containing electro-explosive devices proven by test or analysis to be adversely affected by radio frequency energy to the point that the safety and/or reliability of the system is in jeopardy when the system is employed in its expected radio frequency environment. (JP 1-02. SOURCE: JP 3-04)

**HERO UNSAFE ordnance.** Any ordnance item containing electro-explosive devices that has not been classified as HERO SAFE or HERO SUSCEPTIBLE ordnance as a result of a hazards of electromagnetic radiation to ordnance (HERO) analysis or test is considered HERO UNSAFE ordnance. Additionally, any ordnance item containing electro-explosive devices (including those previously classified as HERO SAFE or HERO SUSCEPTIBLE ordnance) that has its internal wiring exposed; when tests are being conducted on that item that result in additional electrical connections to the item; when electro-explosive devices having exposed wire leads are present and handled or loaded in any but the tested condition; when the item is being assembled or disassembled; or when such ordnance items are damaged causing exposure of internal wiring or components or destroying engineered HERO protective devices. (JP 1-02. SOURCE: JP 3-04)

**hovering.** None. (Approved for removal from JP 1-02.)

**hung ordnance.** Those weapons or stores on an aircraft that the pilot has attempted to drop or fire but could not because of a malfunction of the weapon, rack or launcher, or aircraft release and control system. (JP 1-02. SOURCE: JP 3-04)

**instrument approach procedure.** A series of predetermined maneuvers for the orderly transfer of an aircraft under instrument flight conditions from the beginning of the initial approach to a landing or to a point from which a landing may be made visually or the missed approach procedure is initiated. (JP 1-02. SOURCE: JP 3-04)

**instrument meteorological conditions.** Meteorological conditions expressed in terms of visibility, distance from cloud, and ceiling; less than minimums specified for visual meteorological conditions. Also called **IMC.** (JP 1-02. SOURCE: JP 3-04)

**landing aid.** Any illuminating light, radio beacon, radar device, communicating device, or any system of such devices for aiding aircraft in an approach and landing. (JP 1-02. SOURCE: JP 3-04)

**landing signalman enlisted.** Enlisted man responsible for ensuring that helicopters/tiltrotor aircraft, on signal, are safely started, engaged, launched, recovered, and shut down. Also called **LSE.** (Approved for incorporation into JP 1-02.)

**landing signals officer.** Officer responsible for the visual control of aircraft in the terminal phase of the approach immediately prior to landing. Also called **LSO.** (JP 1-02. SOURCE: JP 3-04)

**lot.** None. (Approved for removal from JP 1-02.)

**multispot ship.** Those ships certified to have two or more adjacent landing areas. (Approved for replacement of "multi-spot ship" in JP 1-02.)

**Naval Air Training and Operating Procedures Standardization manual.** Series of general and specific aircraft procedural manuals that govern the operations of naval aircraft. Also called **NATOPS manual.** (JP 1-02. SOURCE: JP 3-04)

**officer of the deck.** 1. When underway, the officer designated by the commanding officer to be in charge of the ship, including its safe and proper operation. 2. When in port or at anchor, the officer of the deck is designated by the command duty officer, has similar responsibilities, and may be enlisted. Also called **OOD.** (Approved for incorporation into JP 1-02.)

**operational necessity.** A mission associated with war or peacetime operations in which the consequences of an action justify the risk of loss of aircraft and crew. (JP 1-02. SOURCE: JP 3-04)

**ordnance handling.** Applies to those individuals who engage in the breakout, lifting, or repositioning of ordnance or explosive devices in order to facilitate storage or stowage, assembly or disassembly, loading or downloading, or transporting. (Approved for inclusion in JP 1-02.)

**packup kit.** Service-provided maintenance gear sufficient for a short-term deployment, including spare parts and consumables most commonly needed by the deployed helicopter detachment. Supplies are sufficient for a short-term deployment but do not include all material needed for every maintenance task. Also called **PUK.** (Approved for incorporation into JP 1-02.)

**presail.** The time prior to a ship getting under way used to prepare for at-sea events. (JP 1-02. SOURCE: JP 3-04)

**primary flight control.** The controlling agency on air-capable ships that is responsible for air traffic control of aircraft within 5 nautical miles of the ship. On most Coast Guard cutters, primary flight control duties are performed by a combat information center, and the term "PRIFLY" is not used. Also called **PRIFLY.** (Approved for incorporation into JP 1-02.)

**short takeoff and landing.** The ability of an aircraft to clear a 50-foot (15 meters) obstacle within 1,500 feet (450 meters) of commencing takeoff or in landing, to stop within 1,500 feet (450 meters) after passing over a 50-foot (15 meters) obstacle. Also called **STOL.** (Approved for incorporation into JP 1-02 with JP 3-04 as the source JP.)

**short takeoff and vertical landing aircraft.** None. (Approved for removal from JP 1-02.)

**spot.** 1. To determine by observation, deviations of ordnance from the target for the purpose of supplying necessary information for the adjustment of fire. 2. To place in a proper location. 3. An approved shipboard helicopter landing site. (JP 1-02. SOURCE: JP 3-04)

**spotting.** Parking aircraft in an approved shipboard landing site. (JP 1-02. SOURCE: JP 3-04)

**strikedown.** None. (Approved for removal from JP 1-02.)

**transporting (ordnance).** None. (Approved for removal from JP 1-02.)

**vertical replenishment.** The use of a helicopter for the transfer of material to or from a ship. Also called **VERTREP.** (JP 1-02. SOURCE: JP 3-04)

**visual meteorological conditions.** Weather conditions in which visual flight rules apply; expressed in terms of visibility, ceiling height, and aircraft clearance from clouds along the path of flight. Also called **VMC.** (Approved for incorporation into JP 1-02.)

**warning.** None. (Approved for removal from JP 1-02.)

Intentionally Blank

# JOINT DOCTRINE PUBLICATIONS HIERARCHY

JP 1
JOINT DOCTRINE
JP 1-0
PERSONNEL
JP 2-0
INTELLIGENCE
JP 3-0
OPERATIONS
JP 4-0
LOGISTICS
JP 5-0
PLANS
JP 6-0
COMMUNICATIONS SYSTEM


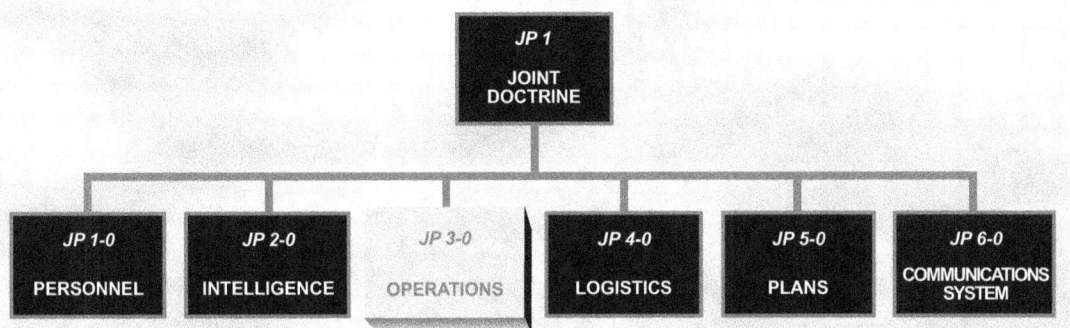

All joint publications are organized into a comprehensive hierarchy as shown in the chart above. **Joint Publication (JP) 3-04** is in the **Operations** series of joint doctrine publications. The diagram below illustrates an overview of the development process:

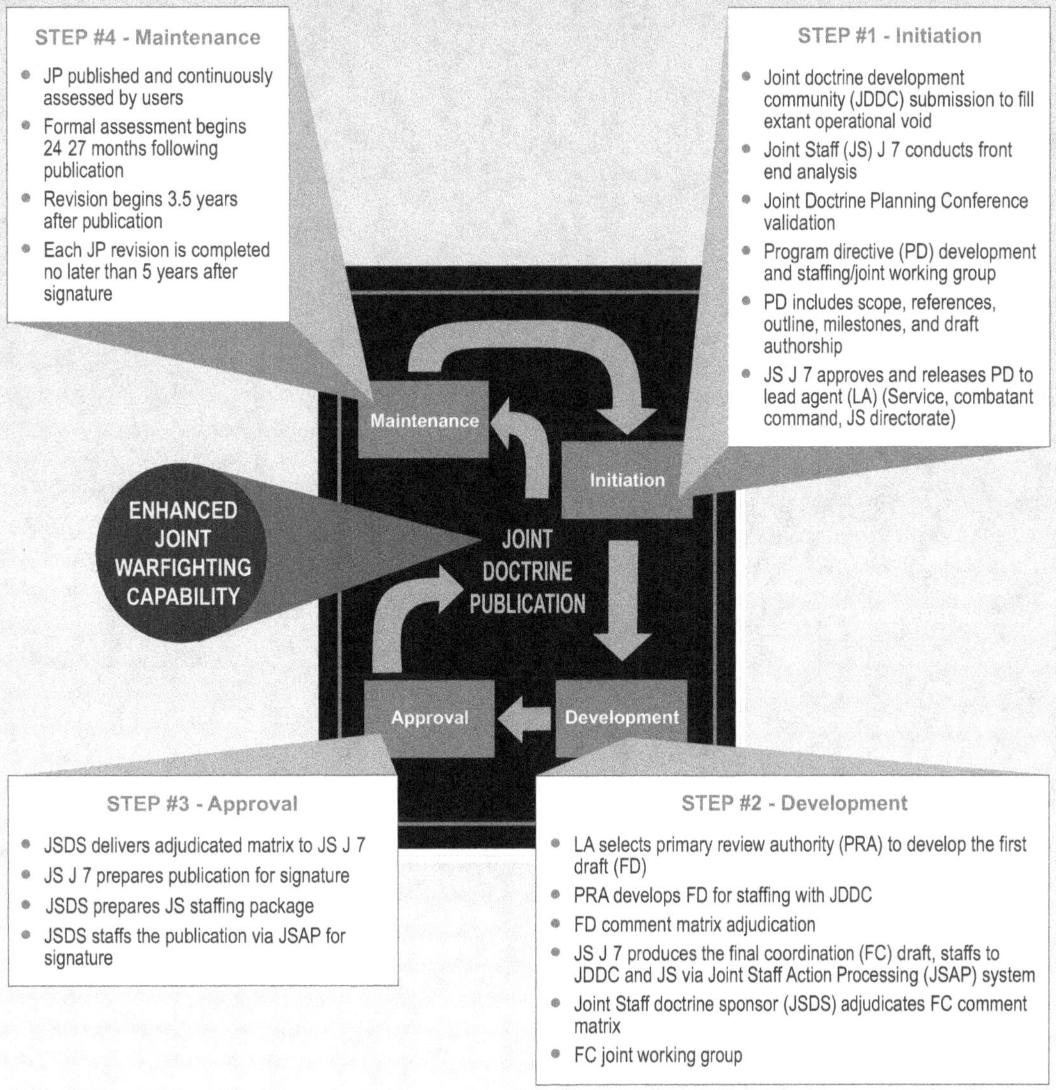

STEP #4 - Maintenance
JP published and continuously assessed by users
Formal assessment begins 24 27 months following publication
Revision begins 3.5 years after publication
Each JP revision is completed no later than 5 years after signature
STEP #1 - Initiation
Joint doctrine development community (JDDC) submission to fill extant operational void
Joint Staff (JS) J 7 conducts front end analysis
Joint Doctrine Planning Conference validation
Program directive (PD) development and staffing/joint working group
PD includes scope, references, outline, milestones, and draft authorship
JS J 7 approves and releases PD to lead agent (LA) (Service, combatant command, JS directorate)
Maintenance
Initiation
ENHANCED JOINT WARFIGHTING CAPABILITY
JOINT DOCTRINE PUBLICATION
Approval
Development
STEP #3 - Approval
JSDS delivers adjudicated matrix to JS J 7
JS J 7 prepares publication for signature
JSDS prepares JS staffing package
JSDS staffs the publication via JSAP for signature
STEP #2 - Development
LA selects primary review authority (PRA) to develop the first draft (FD)
PRA develops FD for staffing with JDDC
FD comment matrix adjudication
JS J 7 produces the final coordination (FC) draft, staffs to JDDC and JS via Joint Staff Action Processing (JSAP) system
Joint Staff doctrine sponsor (JSDS) adjudicates FC comment matrix
FC joint working group